PUBLISHER'S NOTE

Ancient Chinese classic poems are exquisite works of art. As far as 2,000 years ago, Chinese poets composed the beautiful work *Book of Poetry* and *Elegies of the South*. Later, they created more splendid Tang poetry and Song lyrics. Such classic works as *Thus Spoke the Master* and *Laws Divine and Human* were extremely significant in building and shaping the culture of the Chinese nation. These works are both a cultural bond linking the thoughts and affections of Chinese people and an important bridge for Chinese culture and the world.

Mr. Xu Yuanchong has been engaged in translation for 70 years. He won the Lifetime Achievement Award in Translation conferred by the Translators Association of China (TAC) in 2010, and won the "Aurora Borealis" Prize for Outstanding Translation of Fiction Literature, conferred by the Federation of International Translators (FIT) in 2014. He is honored as the only expert who translates Chinese poems into both English and French. After his excellent interpretation, many Chinese classic poems have been further refined into perfect English and French rhymes. This collection of Classical Chinese Poetry and Prose gathers his most representative English translations. It includes the classic works *Thus Spoke the Master, Laws Divine and Human* and dramas such as *Romance of the Western Bower, Dream in Peony Pavilion, Love in Long-life Hall* and *Peach Blooms Painted with Blood*. The largest part of the collection includes the translation of selected poems from different dynasties. The selection includes various types of poetry. The selected works start from the pre-Qin era to the Qing Dynasty, covering almost the entire history of classic poems in China. Reading these works is like tasting "living water from the source" of Chinese culture.

We hope this collection will help English readers "understand, enjoy and delight in" Chinese classic poems, share the intelligence of Confucius and Lao Tzu (the Older Master), share the gracefulness of Tang poems, Song lyrics and classic operas and songs and promote exchanges between Eastern and Western culture. We also sincerely invite precious suggestions from our readers.

出版前言

　　中国古代经典诗文是中国传统文化的奇葩。早在两千多年以前，中国诗人就写出了美丽的《诗经》和《楚辞》；以后，他们又创造了更加灿烂的唐诗和宋词。《论语》《老子》这样的经典著作，则在塑造、构成中华民族文化精神方面具有极其重要的意义。这些作品既是联接所有中国人思想、情感的文化纽带，也是中国文化走向世界的重要桥梁。

　　许渊冲先生从事翻译工作70年，2010年荣获"中国翻译文化终身成就奖"，2014年荣获国际译联颁发的"北极光"杰出文学翻译奖。他被称为将中国诗词译成英法韵文的唯一专家，经他的妙手，许多中国经典诗文被译成出色的英文和法文韵语。这套"许译中国经典诗文集"荟萃许先生最具代表性的英文译作，既包括《论语》《老子》这样的经典著作，又包括《西厢记》《牡丹亭》《长生殿》《桃花扇》等戏曲剧本，数量最多的则是历代诗歌选集。这些诗歌选集包括诗、词、散曲等多种体裁，所选作品上起先秦，下至清代，几乎涵盖了中国古典诗歌的整个历史。阅读和了解这些作品，即可尽览中国文化的"源头活水"。

　　我们希望这套许氏译本能使英语读者对中国经典诗文也"知之，好之，乐之"，能够分享孔子、老子的智慧，分享唐诗、宋词、中国古典戏曲的优美，并以此促进东西文化的交流。也敬请读者朋友提出宝贵意见。

PROJECT FOR TRANSLATION AND PUBLICATION
OF CHINESE CULTURAL WORKS
中国文化著作翻译出版工程项目

CLASSICAL CHINESE POETRY AND PROSE

GOLDEN TREASURY OF CHINESE POETRY IN HAN, WEI AND SIX DYNASTIES

TRANSLATED BY XU YUANCHONG

许译中国经典诗文集

汉魏六朝诗选 | 许渊冲　译

五洲传播出版社　　中　华　书　局
China Intercontinental Press　　Zhonghua Book Company

CONTENTS
目　　录

11

CLASSICAL CHINESE POETRY AND PROSE

GOLDEN TREASURY OF
CHINESE POETRY IN HAN,
WEI AND SIX DYNASTIES

TRANSLATED BY XU YUANCHONG

China Intercontinental Press   Zhonghua Book Company

PREFACE

I

"Chinese literature," said John Turner, "is the artistic peak of the most literary, the most artistic, the longest-established civilization that exists." One source of Chinese literature is the *Book of Poetry* compiled in the 6th century BC, marked by the use of four-character verse form as follows:

> When I left here,
> Willows shed tear.
> I come back now,
> Snow bends the bough.
> Long, long the way;
> Hard, hard the day.
> My grief o'erflows.
> Who knows? Who knows?
> (*A Homesick Warrior*)

Another source is the *Elegies of the South* composed in the 3rd century BC, marked by the use of six-character verse broken in the middle by the insertion of an exclamation such as "oh" or "eh", for example:

> The autumn breeze, oh! ceaselessly grieves
> The Dongting waves, oh! with fallen leaves.

In 206 BC Liu Bang founded the Han Dynasty. In 196 BC he revisited his native village when he composed the *Song of the Great Wind* in the same style as the *Elegies of the South*:

> A great wind rises, oh! the clouds are driven away.

His grandson, Liu Che or Emperor Wu of the Han, who founded in 120 BC the Music Bureau to collect folk songs from various parts of the empire, also wrote in this style:

> The autumn wind rises, oh! and white clouds sail the sky;
>
> Grass and leaves yellow, oh! and wild geese southward fly.
>
> Orchids and asters, oh! sweeten the chilly air;
>
> But how can I forget, oh! my lady sweet and fair!

In this *Song of the Autumn Wind* we see Emperor Wu revealed his love for his deceased Lady Li, of whom we find a good description in her brother's *Song of the Northern Beauty*:

> At her first glance, soldiers would lose their town;
>
> At her second, a monarch would his crown.

This description may be compared with that of Duchess Zhuang Jiang in the *Book of Poetry*:

> Her forehead like a dragonfly's,
>
> Her arched brows curved like a bow.
>
> Ah! dark on white her speaking eyes,
>
> Her cheeks with smiles and dimples glow.

We may say the *Book of Poetry* describes the physical beauty of the Duchess and Lady Li's brother her spiritual beauty. It would be interesting to remark that Li wrote not in the same style as Liu Che but in the folk song style. The folk songs in the *Book of Poetry* are lyrical while those of the Music Bureau are narrative. For instance, we may compare *A Homesick Warrior* cited above with a song of the same title selected in this book.

The folk songs of the Han Dynasty are characterized by the use of lines of irregular length. They reflect the lives and hardships of the common people. Some deal with their miseries (*Song of the East Gate, On Her Deathbed*), evils of war (*Fighting South of the Town*), oppression of feudal society (*Song of the Orphan*), desertion of woman by man (*Song of the White Hair, the Old Wife and The New*) etc. Others deal with love between man and woman (*I Long for One, The Pledge*) and still others with birds and fish (*Song of a Butterfly, Song of a Crow, Song of a Dried Fish*) etc. The most important folk song is *A Pair of Peacocks Southeast Fly*, the longest narrative poem written in five-character lines, telling how the feudal system destroyed the happiness of a young couple who were unable to overcome it unless in death.

Nineteen Old Poems are said to be the earliest folk songs written in the five-character line, for example:

> You travel on and on,
> And leave me all alone.
> Long miles between us lie
> As earth apart from sky.

Some poems deal with love (XVIII. I'll make a quilt for lovers' bed) and marriage (XVII. My far-off husband longs for his dear wife), others with friendship (VII. No friendship is as firm as rock), feasting (IV. We keep a feast in spirits high), or the quest for fame (XI. Let's value glory more than gold) and fortune(III. How splendid is Riverside Town). For the most part they are somber in tone, no doubt reflecting the troubled social conditions of the time, and dwell much on the themes of distance (VI. The one I love is living far away), separation (IX. But I'm grieved so long we've parted), and the dreadful brevity (XV. Few live as long as a hundred years) and uncertainty of human life (XIII. Life is a journey which can never last/As long as stone or metal).

In short, just as the *Book of Poetry* is marked by the use of four character verse and the *Poetry of the South* by that of six-character line broken in the middle by the insertion of an exclamation, the Han poetry is marked by the rise of the five-character verse which would exercise a great influence on later Chinese poetry.

II

Chinese history was marked by unification, division and reunification. Liu Bang unified the country and built up his empire in 206 BC, but the Han Dynasty fell in AD 220 and the empire split into the three kingdoms of Wei in the north, Shu in the west and Wu in the south with its capital at Jiankang (modern Nanjing). The dynasty of Wei was set up by Cao Cao (155–220), who was not only a military leader but also a poet who followed the tradition of the *Book of Poetry* and continued to write in the old four-character verse form.

Cao Pi(187–226), his eldest son who succeeded him on the throne and forced the last emperor of Han Dynasty to abdicate followed the tradition of the *Poetry of the South* but turned the inserted exclamation in the middle of the six-character line into a word or character so that he became the first poet to write in the seven-character line. For instance, we may read the first four lines of his *Lonely Wife* in the North:

> The weather turns cold when bleak blows the autumn breeze;
>
> The leaves shiver and fall; into frost dewdrops freeze.
>
> Swallows in group fly south together with wild geese;
>
> Missing you so far off, my heart is not at ease.

It would be interesting to compare this song with *The Sea* of his father. Both of them talked about the bleak autumn wind, but the father thought of "the monstrous billows" surging up high, and of his own lofty aspiration, while the son became sympathetic with a lonely wife, and thought of a peaceful home life. What is true of father and son is equally true of the first

Emperor of Han dynasty and his grandson Emperor Wu.

Emperors and kings, ministers and generals, all were poets bred in the same tradition, in the folk songs of the common people. That is the reason why Chinese literature is said to be "the longest-established civilization that exists."

Cao Zhi (192–232), the third son of Cao Cao, was well-known for his literary talent, especially for his five-character verse. He won the favor of his father at the age of ten and lost that of his eldest brother, who became later the first emperor of Wei and ordered him, under pain of death, to write a poem within the time of taking seven paces. And he did write the following quatrain:

> Pods burned to cook peas,
> Peas weep in the pot.
> "Grown from the same trees,
> Why boil us so hot?"

This symbolic poem saved his life as well as his literary renown. In his *Song of a Beauty* we find the following:

> Her melting glance reveals her shining eye;
> In her sweet breath you hear the orchid sigh,
> She lives alone at her prime, fair and bright.
> How can she not sigh at the dead of night!

If we compare his *Beauty* with his brother's *Lonely Wife*, we may find Cao Pi objective and sympathetic and Cao Zhi subjective and symbolic. The lonely wife sighed because her husband was far off, and the poet was merely sympathetic with her. The beauty sighed because she was not married at her prime just as the poet was not employed at his because his brother, suspicious of his disloyalty, would persecute him to death. So the beauty was symbolic of the poet himself.

Besides the three Caos, the most important poet of the Wei was Ruan Ji (210–263), well-known for his satirical *Reflections*:

> (III) Bright flowers languish soon and fade;
>> With thorns the hall will be overgrown.
> (VI) The plain-dressed may live to the end;
>> On royal favor none can depend.

His poems may rival with Cao Zhi's but they are ambiguous.

In short, the Wei poetry is marked by the rise of the seven-character verse form which has exercised as great an influence on later poetry as the five-character verse of the Han.

III

In 280 the three kingdoms were reunified by the Jin Dynasty (265–420). The Confucian doctrines that had formed the official foundation of the Han Dynasty were in some degree discredited with the decay and collapse of the Han and interest in the transcendental thought of Taoist philosophy revived. The poet well-known for his Taoist ideas was Guo Pu (276–324), in whose *Songs of Immortals* we find the following verse:

> The gallants live in capital;
> The hermits' huts in forest stand.
> Why should you envy lordly hall
> Not lasting as the fairy land? ...
> Better soar over the world in breeze
> And overdo the hermits with ease!

During the Jin Dynasty most scholars tried to escape reality and the best known poet was Tao Qian (or Tao Yuanming 365–427), who retired from official life to a pastoral one of farming and writing and became the archetype of the "hermit poet" at the foot of the famous Mount Lu, the "Southern Hill "as he mentioned in the following verse:

> I pick fence side chrysanthemums at will;
>
> Carefree, I see the Southern Hill.
>
> The mountain air is fresh day and night;
>
> Together birds go home in flight.

Lines 1 and 2 are representative of the poet's love of nature and freedom. The aster or chrysanthemum, the last cold-proof flower to bloom in autumn, is the symbol of purity in difficult circumstances and the Southern Hill, that of tranquillity, longevity and eternity. Therefore, the poet's love of aster and hill reveals his own character, pure and cold-proof as the one and tranquil and lasting as the other.

In line 4 the birds' flight symbolizes the poet's life journey and its homecoming alludes to his return to his native land. These four lines sum up the pursuit, frustration, retreat and self-cultivation of an intellectual in troubled times.

Many of Tao's poems described the quiet joys of country life (*Return to Nature, Moving House*), though others spoke of famine, drought and similar hardships (*Begging for Food, A Poor Scholar*).

The Taoist side of his nature told him he should be content with such a life of seclusion (Secluded heart creates secluded plan), but his dedication to Confucian ideals kept him longing for the less troubled times of the past when virtue prevailed and a scholar could in good conscience take an active part in state affairs, as shown in his four-character verse *Spring Excursion* written in the style of the *Book of Poetry*:

> I gaze mid-stream
>
> And miss the sages

> Singing their dream
> Of Golden Ages.
> How I adore
> Their quiet day!
> Their time's no more
> And gone for aye.

The sages in the above poem referred to Confucius and his disciples. Unable to attain his ideal, he sought solace in wine and verse (*Drinking Wine*).

In a word, the Jin poetry is marked by Tao Qian's pastoral or hermit poems. On the other hand, *Spirit of the Four Seasons* written by the famous painter Gu Kaizhi(345–406) on four of his pictures may be said to be the forerunner of landscape or "mountain and river" poetry of the Southern Dynasties:

> Spring water overbrims the streams;
> Summer cloud fancy peaks outshines;
> The autumn moon sheds brilliant beams;
> On winter cliffs stand cold –proof pines.

IV

In 265 the Jin Dynasty reunited the empire, but soon it fell victim to internal dissention and invasion from the north. In time, both the western and eastern capitals (Chang'an and Luoyang) had fallen to Northern tribes, and in 317 the Jin emperor and his court fled to the southern capital Jiankang (modern Nanjing), the dynasty thereafter being known as the Eastern Jin. For nearly three centuries, roughly the period known as the Six Dynasties, the north remained in the hands of the Northern rulers, while a succession of weak dynasties ruled the south, known as the Southern Dynasties: Song

(420−479), Qi (479−501), Liang (501−557) and Chen (557−589).

Liu Yu (reigned 420−422), founder of the Song dynasty, was glorified as "the Cowherd King" by a later poet Xin Qiji (1140−1207) in his lyric written to the tune of *Joy of Eternal Union*:

Where lived the Cowherd King retaking the lost land.

In bygone years,

Leading armed cavaliers,

With golden spear in hand,

Tiger-like, he had slain

The foe in Central Plain.

The most important poet of the Song Dynasty was Xie Lingyun (385−433). Noted for his rapt appreciation of the sights of nature, he was often looked on as the father of landscape or "mountain and river" poetry. He was well-known for the following verse:

High mountains spread for miles and miles;

The stream is dotted with isles and isles.

White clouds embrace the boulders steep;

Green ripples lull bamboos to sleep.

He was considered as a better poet than Tao Qian in his time. His verse is balanced and elaborate while Tao's style is plain and simple. His is an objective description of mountain and stream while Tao's is an subjective one in which the outer world and his inner world mingle and become one. That is the reason why later poets considered Tao better than Xie. However, both their poetry exercised great influence on Tang poet Wang Wei (701−761).

Another important Song poet was Bao Zhao (415−470). His verse exercised influence on great Tang poets Li Bai (701−762)and Gao Shi (706−765). Li wrote *Hard Is the Way* in imitation of his *Hard Is The Way* and Gao wrote *Song of the Northern Frontier* in imitation of his song of the same title. For instance, we may read the following verse:

> A man's life's also ruled by fate.
>
> Why must we sigh outdoors or in, early or late?
>
> Drink wine to drown grief if you may,
>
> And raise your cup and stop to sing the Weary Way.
>
> *(Hard Is The Way)*

> In hard times we see men steadfast;
>
> In chaos we know heroes great.
>
> For good rulers lives may be east
>
> And sacrificed to their dear State.
>
> *(Song of Northern Frontier)*

The most important poet of the Qi Dynasty was Xie Tiao or Junior Xie (464–499). His verse is more natural and less elaborate than Xie Lingyun or Senior Xie's. He is well-known for the following couplet:

> The colored clouds spread like brocade;
>
> The river's clear as silver braid.

Li Bai himself wrote in his verse:

> Mine is in Junior Xie's direct and easy style.

Xiao Yan (464–549), founder of the Liang Dynasty, was himself a poet who began to write palace poems such as

> The morning sun shines on window green;
>
> The breeze ripples embroidered screen.
>
> Her pearllike teeth smile sweet and tender;
>
> Her eyes bewitch with eyebrows slender.

His *Song of the Southern Shore* was said to be the earliest lyric or tuned poem.

The most important Liang poet was Shen Yue (441–512), credited with having laid down the principles for tonal regulations of poetry. The tonally regulated verse form did not reach full maturity till the Tang Dynasty (618–907). Besides, Shen was well-known for his *Six Recollections*:

> I think of when she came
> Up marble steps like bright, bright flame.
> Talking long, long of when we parted,
> Of sad, sad yearning, broken-hearted.

Another important Liang poet was He Xun (?–518), who exercised influence on great Tang poet Du Fu(712–770). For instance, we may read his *Reply to Fan Yun*:

> My cot is shaded with leafy trees;
> Lush grass would darken doorsteps quiet.
> Bright blooms caressed by gentle breeze,
> Sunbeams amid flowers run riot.

If we compare the first two lines with the following verse of Du Fu:

> Around the steps in vain spring has tinged grass green;
> Amid thick leaves to no avail the orioles sing.
>
> *(The Temple of the Famous Premier of Shu)*

We can see how the great Tang poet learned from his master and excelled him.

Yu Xin (512–580) was also a Liang poet who became a captive of the Northern emperor and served in the Northern court. That is the reason why he was considered as a poet of Northern Dynasties. In his verse we often find nostalgic thoughts, for example, in *Parting Again with Secretary Zhou*:

> On long, long way of Sunny Pass
> Alone I can't go back, alas!
> Only the riverside wild geese

> Fly southward when blows autumn breeze.

His verse also exercised great influence on Li Bai and was considered as an important forerunner of Tang poetry.

As the founder of the Liang Dynasty, the last emperor of the Chen (553–604)was also a poet, notorious for his *Blooming Jade Trees in the Backyard* because he was hearing this song when the Sui army entered his capital and he was made a captive. Hence this song became the symbol of a conquered kingdom. Du Mu (803–852) wrote about it in his well-known verse:

> The songstress, knowing not the grief of conquered land,
>
> Still sings the song composed by a captive ruler's hand.

Another important Chen poet was Yin Keng (?–565). Du Fu said in his verse that he learned to write poetry from Yin Keng and He Xun. Read Yin's *Leaving New Tower at Dusk*:

> The great river rolls on with ease;
>
> My parting grief surges without rest. ...
>
> Drumbeats are heard from far away;
>
> Pine trees are seen on mountains cold.

And we can see these two couplets are well balanced, and that is perhaps what Du Fu learned from his master in writing his regulated verse.

Different from this regulated verse are anonymous poems called *Midnight Songs* written by Southern singing girls. Among them are love songs, pert in tone, lively and colloquial in language, often employing puns to add an innuendo to the surface meaning. The most important folk song in the Southern Dynasties was *Song of the Western Islet*, of which the theme is the lovesickness a maiden revealed in a series of activities conscious or unconscious, so this poem may be said to be the first subconscious verse in Chinese history. The most important folk song in the Northern Dynasties was *Song of Mulan*, Joand' Arc in Chinese literature. In this poem her military life is narrated only in six short lines and her homecoming in twenty-two, which proves that the Chinese poet is not so much interested in describing heroic deeds and adventures as human feelings and characters.

V

In 589 General Yang Jian unified the Northern and the Southern Dynasties and founded the Sui (589-618), a shortlived dynasty that prepared the way for the more lasting Tang. Yang Guang (569-618), its second and last emperor, notorious for his luxurious life, was not a bad poet nevertheless. Read his *Field View*:

> Here and there fly a thousand dots of crows;
>
> Around a lonely village water flows.
>
> The slanting sun bids to the day adieu.
>
> How can my heart not break at this sad view?

This poem seemed to predict the downfall of the Sui Dynasty. A later poet Qin Guan (1049-1100)reversed this poem in his lyric as follows:

> Beyond the setting sun I see but dots of crows
>
> And that around a lonely village water flows.

From this we can see how Chinese poetic tradition passed the Han, Wei, Jin, Song, Qi, Liang, Chen and Sui dynasties to the Tang and the Song, her Golden and Silver Ages.

Xu Yuanchong
July 24, 1995

Liu Bang[1] (256–195 BC)

SONG OF THE GREAT WIND

A great wind rises, oh! the clouds are driven away.

I come to my native land, oh! now the world is under my sway.

Where can I find brave men, oh! to guard my four frontiers today!

---

[1] The first emperor of the Han Dynasty (206 BC–AD 220).

Xiang Yu[1] (232–202 BC)

XIANG YU'S LAST SONG

I could pull mountains down, oh! with main and might,

But my good fortune wanes, oh! my steed won't fight.

Whether my steed will fight, oh! I do not care.

What can I do with you, oh! my lady fair!

---

[1] Xiang Yu, the conqueror fought against Liu Bang for the throne. Defeated, he and his favorite Lady Yu committed suicide. The lady was so beautiful that her name became a tune title: "The Beautiful Lady Yu."

Lady Yu[1] (?-202 BC)

REPLY TO XIANG YU

The foes have overrun our land;

From all around they sing our song.

With might and main my lord can't stand,

Could a frail woman turn out strong![2]

---

[1] See note to Xiang Yu. The authenticity of this song is doubtful.

[2] Another version: Need I, a frail woman, live long?

Liu Che[1] (156-87 BC)

SONG OF THE AUTUMN WIND

The autumn wind rises, oh! and white clouds sail the sky;

Grass and leaves yellow, oh! and wild geese southward fly.

Orchids and asters, oh! sweeten the chilly air;

But how can I forget, oh! my lady sweet and fair!

We sail pavilion boat, oh! across the river long;

We reach the mid-stream, oh! and see the breakers white.

The flutes are played and drums, oh! beat time to rowers' song.

But sorrow would arrive, oh! when pleasures reach their height.

How long will youth endure, oh! when old age is in sight!

---

[1] Emperor Wu of the Han Dynasty, who wrote this elegy for his favorite Lady Li.

Sima Xiangru[1] (179–118 BC)

SONGS OF THE LUTE

O phoenix, O phoenix! I come to my homeland
After roaming over the four seas for a mate.
How can I help it, oh! when none is near at hand!
Now I come to this hall, oh! can I anticipate?
There is in the boudoir a maiden nice and fair;
Though near, she is beyond my reach, which breaks my heart.
How can we lie together like lovebirds in pair?
Can we go up and down, oh! and never fly apart?

---

① The authenticity of these two songs is doubtful.

Li Yannian[1] (?–87 BC)

SONG OF THE NORTHERN BEAUTY

There is a beauty in the northern lands;
Unequaled, high above the world she stands.
At her first glance, soldiers would lose their town;
At her second, a monarch would his crown.
How could the soldiers and monarch neglect their duty?
For town and crown are overshadowed by her beauty.

---

① Elder brother of Lady Li, favorite of Emperor Wu (See Note to Liu Che).

Lady Ban[①]

TO AN AUTUMN FAN

Fresh from the weaver's loom, Oh silk so white,

You are as clear as frost, as snow as bright.

Fashioned into a fan, token of love,

You are as round as brilliant moon above.

In my lord's sleeve when in or out he goes,

You wave and shake, and a gentle breeze blows.

I am afraid when comes the autumn day,

And chilling wind drives summer heat away,

You'll be discarded to a lonely place,

And with my lord you'll fall into disgrace.

---

① The favorite of Emperor Cheng, who fell into disgrace like the autumn fan, which has become a symbol of disgrace since then.

Xin Yannian

CAPTAIN OF THE GUARD

In bygone days General Huo had high fame;

He had a slave called Feng Zidu by name.

Relying on the general's full power,

Feng ogled a Hunnish maiden, wine-house flower.

The Hunnish maiden was only fifteen;

Alone she served out wine when spring was green.

Her long gown girt with double girdle by the side,

Her vest adorned with love-birds and sleeves wide.

Jade from Blue Field in her hair did appear;

A pair of Roman pearls behind her ear.

Her two tresses were so charming and fair

That in the world they stood without compare.

One tress was worth five million coins even then;

The two of them were worth much more than ten.

"Who would have thought a captain of the guard

Would drop in and pay me his high regard!

His silver saddle has a dazzling sheen;

His carriage waits with a canopy green.

He comes forward to ask me for clear wine;

I raise jade wine-pot by silken cord fine.

He asks me then for delicious dish;

I offer him on golden plate sliced fish.

He gives me a bronze mirror of renown
And tries to tie it to my red silk gown.
But I would rather have my red silk torn
Than let him stain my body humbly born.
A man would always love a second wife;
A woman should love her husband through life.
The new will come forth if the old should go;
The high cannot be mixed up with the low.
I thank the captain of the Royal Guard:
Please do not press a worthless one too hard!"

Su Wu (140–60 BC)

SU WU TO HIS WIFE

As man and wife we ever unite;
We never doubt about our love.
Let us enjoy our fill tonight
As tender as a cooing dove!
Thinking of the way I should go,
I rise to see if time is due.
The stars appear dim high and low;
Adieu! I must bid you adieu,
Away to battlefield I'll hie;
I know not if we'll meet again.
Holding your hand, I give a sigh;
My tears of farewell fall like rain.
Enjoy the spring flowers in view!
Do not forget our time in glee!
Safe and sound, I'll come back to you;
Even killed, my love won't die with me.

Anonymous

FIGHTING SOUTH OF THE TOWN

Fighting south of the town,

Men were killed up and down.

On those unburied in the wilds crows might be fed,

But I would tell the crows to cry first for the dead:

"Unburied, they're exposed to view.

How can their carrion escape you?"

Clear, clear streams sigh;

Dark, dark reeds sway.

Brave horsemen die;

Wounded steeds neigh.

How to build on the plain

Bridge and house north and south?

When we can reap nor corn nor grain,

With what to feed the monarch's mouth?

O how can we be then

Subjects loyal to His Majesty?

Think of those loyal men

Who are worthy of our memory!

They went out in the morn to fight

But never to come back at night!

I LONG FOR ONE

I long for one who has left me
And gone to the south of the sea.
What shall I send to him as gift?
A pearled comb made
Of tortoise-shell ornated with jade.
When told he is untrue, I'm ill at ease.
I break and rift
The comb, I shatter
It and burn it and scatter
Its ashes to the breeze.
From now on I will never
Think of him who will sever
From me. But how can I forget the night
When barking dogs or cockcrow might
Awake my brother and his wife? I sigh and wail.
To what avail?
I hear the autumn wind so shrill
And pheasants trill,
But soon the sun will rise
And shine in eastern skies.

THE PLEDGE^①

Oh Heaven high!
I will love him forever till I die,
Till mountains crumble ,
Rivers run dry,
In winter thunder rumble,
In summer snow fall far and nigh,
And the earth mingle with the sky,
Not till then will my love die.

---

① This song is said to be the second part of the preceding one.

GATHERING LOTUS

Let's gather lotus seed by southern rivershore!
The lotus sways with teeming leaves we adore.
Among the leaves fish play and make love.
In the east they make love below and we above;
In the west they make love below and we above;
In the south they make love below and we above;
In the north they make love below and we above.^①

---

① The last four lines are refrain sung by four groups.

EAST OF THE TOMB

East of the Tomb

In pine trees' gloom,

Who has carried away our honest groom?

Our groom without resources

Carried to the high hall by forces,

To be ransomed by million coins and two fine horses.

One fine horse, one fine steed,

It's hard indeed.

Seeing the officer, his heart would bleed.

His bleeding heart grows cold.

"Oh let my wife be told:

The yellow calf be sold, the yellow calf be sold!"

THE ROADSIDE MULBERRY

In the southeast rises the sun;
It shines on the House of Qin where
Lives a beauty second to none,
Who calls herself Luofu the fair.
Silkworms with mulberry are fed;
She picks its leaves in southern nook.
Her basket bound with blue silk thread,
Of laurel twig she'd made a hook.
Her "falling" chignon black like jade,
Like moonbeams her pearl ear-rings shine.
Of yellow silk her apron's made,
Her cloak of purple damask fine.
When wayfarers see her pass by,
They put loads down and stroke their beard,
Young men would stare with open eyes
And doff caps to show she's revered.
The plowmen would forget their plows;
The hoers forget the hoes they wield.
At their wives they knit angry brows,
Not so fair as Luofu afield.

From the south comes the governor;
His cab and five steeds won't go on.

He sends forward an officer
To ask who she is, fair as swan.
"I am a daughter of the Qins;
And I'm called Luofu by my kins."
"How old are you?" "Not yet a score,
But I'm more than fifteen, much more."
The lord comes then to ask Luofu,
"Will you please ride with me, will you?"
Luofu steps forth and makes reply:
"What nonsense you are talking! Why!
Your Excellency has his wife;
I have my husband dear for life.

"There're in the east a thousand steeds
And horsemen whom my husband leads.
How can you know my husband bright?
A black colt follows his horse white,
Whose tail is tied with a blue thread,
With golden halters round its head.
He wears a sword with hilt of jade,
For which its weight in gold was paid.
At fifteen he was junior clerk;
At twenty he did courtier's work;

At thirty in chamberlain's gown,
At forty he's lord of a town.
His face is fair, his skin is white,
His hair is fine, his beard is slight.
He walks in the hall at slow pace
And goes to the palace with grace.
'Mid thousands come from east and west,
All say my husband is the best."

A Slow Song

The mallow in the garden green in hue
Awaits the sun to dry the morning dew.
The radiant spring spreads its nourishing light;
All living things become then fresh and bright.
I dread the coming of the autumn drear
When leaves turn yellow and red flowers sere.
A hundred streams flow eastwards to the sea,
When to return to the west can they be free?
If one does not make good use of his youth,
In vain will he pass his old age in ruth.

SONG OF THE EAST GATE

Out of East Gate,

He won t come back.

Now back again,

He finds the lack

Of rice in the pot,

And coat on the peg.

With pain

He grieves,

Sword in hand, he starts out; his wife

Clutches at his sleeves

And weeps to beg

Him not

To risk his life.

"Others for wealth may care;

Your gruel I would share.

For Heaven above,

For our unweaned baby we love,

Please do not go!"

"Bah! it's already late.

Shall we drag on till white hairs grow?"

A Longing Wife

Green, green the grass by riverside;
Long, long I miss him far and wide.
He's far away beyond the stream;
Yet I saw him last night in dream.
I dreamed we side by side did stand;
I woke to find him in far land.
The land's too far to trace the ground;
I tossed but he could not be found.
A withered tree can feel the breeze;
The sea feels cold though it won't freeze.
When men come home, with their wives they feel glad.
Who'd talk with me and care if I feel sad?
But a stranger comes from afar;
He brings me a pair of fine carp.
I call my boy to cook the fish,
In which I find a message as I wish.
I kneel to read what my husband does write
In this dear letter on silk white.
He starts: "Take of your health good care,"
And ends: "I'll think of you fore'er!"

ON HER DEATHBED

A wife's been ill for years;
She calls her husband, but before she speaks
A word, her tears
Stream down her cheeks.
"I'll leave you our child of two years old.
Don't let him go hungry or cold!
Do not beat him if he does wrong,
Or he cannot live long!
Bear it in mind always!"

After her death, her husband says:
"I want to carry my child to the town,
But he has not a gown.
His jacket is too thin;
I have to leave him in.
I close the door and window bare,
And go alone to the fair.
Meeting a friend on the way, I sit down
And weep so much that I can't rise.
With tearful eyes
I beg my friend to buy a cake
For the motherless orphan's sake.
Speaking to him, I can't refrain
From shedding tears in rain.

I will not show my grief but I weep without end,
And I take money from my pocket for my friend.
I come home again for a rest,
And see my son cry for his mother's breast.
I walk in empty room to and fro.
He'll be like this whether I stay or go.
What can I do but leave him in the woe!"

SONG OF A ROAMER

The swallows flit before the hall,
In summer come, in winter go.
Like my brothers from spring to fall,
I roam in strange land high and low.
Who'd patch my worn-out clothes old?
And who will sew the new for me?
The mistress good of the household
Takes and mends my clothes charge-free.
Her husband comes home from afar;
He casts on us suspicious look.
"Do not be jealous as you are!
Pebbles are seen in a clear brook."
My heart's brook-clear where'er I roam;
I find still there's no place like home.

SONG OF THE WHITE HAIR

Our love like snow on mountains proud
Was bright like the moon 'mid the cloud.
I'm told you'll leave the old for new;
I come to say goodbye to you.
We drink a cup of wine today;
Tomorrow we'll go each our way.
By royal moat we'll walk and go
Like waters which east or west flow.
Why should I feel so sad and drear
And like a bride shed tear on tear?
If I'd wed one with single heart,
Even white-haired, we would not part.
Long, long may be your fishing lines,
You cannot catch fishtail which shines.
If your love were constant and true,
Why so much money to go through?

SONG OF A BUTTERFLY

I am a butterfly roaming all over
The eastern garden among the clover.
Surprised and caught by a swallow foraging
For her fledglings in spring.
I'm carried into purple palace deep.
She wheels around the capital
Of pillar tall.
With joy her fledglings hop and leap
At sight of the food she brings;
They crane their necks and flap their wings.

SONG OF A CROW

A crow with fledglings nests on cassia tree
In the yard of the Qin family. Ah me!
There is a reckless son within family walls,
Armed with strong sling-shot and embaumed balls.
Two balls in his left hand, he circles east and west
Around the fledglings' nest. Ah me!
He deals a blow
And hits the crow.
When the mother bird dies,
Her soul flies to the skies.

When she fed her fledglings' mouth,

They lived among the boulders in the south. Ah me!

How could people know where they did stay?

None to their nest could find the winding way.

White deer in Western Royal Garden wide

Are bagged by archers for venison dried. Ah me!

The palace cooks wild swans which flew so high

As to scrape the vault of the sky.

The carp may hide in River Luo's deepest nook;

Its mouth cannot escape the fishing hook. Ah me!

Men may live long or short, different is their fate.

Then why complain if death comes soon or late!

SONG OF A DRIED FISH

A dried fish weeps, ferried across the stream;

Already caught now, he repents too late.

He writes a letter to the tench and bream,

Warning them to be wary of the bait.

A Song of Grief

I sing a song of grief: it is my tears;
I gaze afar, but no homeland appears.
I dream of native village still,
Of tree on tree and hill on hill.
I'll go home where no kinsfolk can I see;
I'll cross the stream, no boat will ferry me.
To whom can I tell what I feel?
My heart seems ground by rolling wheel.

A Pair of Peacocks Southeast Fly

During the reign of Jian'an (196–219) in the Eastern Han Dynasty there
was a local official in the prefecture of Lujiang called Jiao Zhongqing, whose
wife, Liu Lanzhi, was sent away by his mother and vowed never to marry
again. Compelled by her family to break her vow, she had no recourse
but to drown herself in a pool. On hearing the news, Zhongqing hanged
himself on a tree in the courtyard. The following poem was composed by
contemporaries in their memory.

A pair of peacocks southeast fly;
At each mile they look back and cry.
"I could weave," said Lanzhi, at thirteen
And learned to cut clothes at fourteen;

At fifteen to play music light;

At sixteen to read and to write.

At seventeen to you I was wed.

What an austere life have led!

"You're an official far away;

I toil as housewife night and day.

At daybreak I begin to weave;

At night the loom I dare not leave.

I've finished five rolls in three days,

Yet I am blamed for my delays.

Not that my work is done too slow,

But hard your housewife's role does grow.

If Mother thinks I am no good,

What use to stay, although I would?

Will you come and to Mother say,

Send me back home without delay?"

Jiao Zhongqing came home at her call

And said to his mother in the hall,

"I'm destined for a humble life;

By fortune I have this good wife.

We've shared the pillow, mat and bed,

And we'll be man and wife till dead.

We've lived together but three years,

Which not too long to me appears.

She has done nothing wrong, I find.
Why should you be to her unkind?"
His mother said then in reply,
"You are indeed shortsighted. Why?
This wife of yours with me goes ill;
She always does whate'er she will.
I've been offended by her for long.
How dare you say she's done no wrong?
In the east there's a match for you,
A maiden whose name's Qin Luofu,
A peerless beauty of this land.
I'll go for you to ask her hand.
Now send your slut out of our door!
She should not stay here any more."
Zhongqing knelt down with trunk erect
And said to her with due respect,
"If you should send away my wife,
I won't remarry all my life."
The mother was angry at his word;
Her strumming on the stool was heard.
"Has filial reverence come to nil?
Defend your wife against my will!
You are such an ungrateful son!
Of your request I will grant none."

Zhongqing dared not speak any more,
But bowed and entered his own door.
He tells his wife when she appears,
His voice choked so with bitter tears,
"Not that I would send you away,
But Mother won't allow you to stay.
Return to your brother's house, So
That to my office I may go.
When I have finished my work, Then
I'll come and fetch you home again.
Do not be grieved to say adieu,
But keep in mind what I've told you!"
"Nay, make no care to come for me!"
To her husband addresses she.
"One early spring day, I recall,
I left home for your entrance hall.
I've done what Mother ordered me.
Dare I be careless and carefree?
I do hard labour day and night;
Alone I toil with all my might.
I think I have done nothing wrong,
Still with Mother I can't get along.
To what avail to talk about
Returning now I'm driven out!
I'll leave my jacket of brocade,

Whose lacings bright of gold are made,
And my canopy of gauze red,
Whose four corners with perfume spread,
And sixty trunks and coffers tied
With silken threads all in green dyed,
Where different things you will find;
Not two of them are of a kind.
They are as cheap as I, it's true,
Not good enough for your spouse new.
So as gifts you may share them out,
As we can't meet again, no doubt.
Keep them in memory of me!
Forgetful we can never be."

At dawn she rose at the cockcrow
And made up with care, ready to go.
She put on an embroidered gown
And checked it over, up and down.
She put on shoes made of brocade,
Of tortoise shell her hairpin's made.
Her waist was girt with girdle white,
Her ear-rings shone like moonlight bright.
She had tapering finger tips,
Like rubies were her rouged lips.
She moved at slow and easy pace,

Unrivalled in the human race.
She came to his mother in the hall,
Who said no tender words at all.
"While young, before I was a spouse,
I lived but in a country house.
Not well instructed or wide read,
For noble heir I was ill-bred.
Though kindly you have treated me,
Yet I'm not dutiful, " said she,
"So I must go back in despair,
Leaving to you all household care."
She said to his sister good-byes,
Bitter tears trickled from her eye.
"When your brother and I were wed,
You came around our nuptial bed.
You are as tall as I today,
When I am to be driven away.
Take good care of your mother old,
and take good care of your household!
When maidens hold their festive day,
Do not forget me while you play."
She went out and got on the cart;
Tears streamed down, heavy was her heart.

Jiao Zhongqing rides before, his mind

Turning to his wife's cart behind.
The cart's rumble's heard to repeat.
The husband stops where four roads meet.
He gets down from his horse, comes near
His wife and whispers in her ear,
"I swear not to leave you long, my spouse.
Return now to your brother's house.
When I have finished my work, then
I'll come and fetch you home again.
I swear to heaven high above,
That forever will last our love."
Lanzhi says to her husband dear,
"I'm touched by your love sincere.
If I'm engraved deep in your mind,
Come then in time and not behind!
If as the rock your love is strong,
Then mine as creeping vine is long.
The vine's resistant as silk thread;
No one could lift a rock o'erhead.
But my brother's temper is hot,
Look on me kindly he will not.
I am afraid he'll never care
What I like, and it's hard to bear."
They wave their hands with broken heart,
From each other they will not part.

Lanzhi came to her mother's place,
Feeling embarrassed in disgrace.
Her mother clapped loud in surprise:
"How can you come back in this guise!
You were taught to weave at thirteen;
To cut the clothes at fourteen;
At fifteen to play music light;
At sixteen to perform the rite.
At seventeen you were a bride;
By your husband you should abide.
Had you done nothing wrong at all,
Why come back alone to my hall?"
Lanzhi told her mother the truth,
Who was moved to tears, full of ruth.

She had been back many a day,
A go-between then came to say,
"Our magistrate has a third son,
Whose good looks are second to none.
Though at eighteen or nineteen years,
For eloquence he has no peers."
Her mother said to her, "Consent
to this proposal benevolent!"
But she only answered in tears,
"Can I forget my married years?

My husband vowed when we parted then,
Never should we sever again.
If I should break my word today,
Would regret for e'er and aye.
Will you please tell the go-between
Gently and clearly what I mean?"
Her mother told the messenger,
"This humble daughter of mine, sir,
Sent back by an official of late,
Can't match a son of magistrate.
Why not inquire another house
Where may be found a better spouse?"

No sooner had gone this messenger,
Than came one from the governor.
"You have a daughter fair," said he,
"Of an official's family.
Our governor has a fifth son,
Unmarried, he's a handsome one.
My lord's secretary asked me
His lordship's go-between to be.
I was told to say openly.
I come for my lord's family.
His son will have your daughter for spouse.
That's why I'm sent to your noble house."

Mother Liu thanked the messenger,

But said she could not order her

Who'd made a vow, to break her word.

By Lanzhi's brother this was heard;

As it troubled his worldly mind,

He spoke to Lanzhi words unkind.

"Why don't you, sister, think it over?

You left then an official's door;

Now you may marry a noble son;

Good luck comes when bad luck is done.

If you refuse this honour great,

I don't know what will be your fate."

Lanzhi replied, raising her head,

"Brother, it's right what you have said.

I left you once to be a spouse;

Sent back, again I'm in your house.

So I'm at your disposal now,

Can I do what you don't allow?

Though I vowed to my husband dear,

We cannot meet again, I fear.

So you may marry me at will,

My obligation I'll fulfil."

The go-between learned what they said,

To his lord's house he went ahead.

He said his errand was well done;

The lord rejoiced for his fifth son.
He found in the almanac soon,
The auspicious date of that moon.
He said to his subordinate,
"The thirtieth day is the best date.
That is only three days ahead.
Arrange the marriage in my stead."
The lord's order was given loud;
People bustled like floating Cloud.
They painted with bird designs the boat
And with dragons the flags afloat.
A golden cab with wheels trimmed with jade
And golden saddles for steeds were made.
Three thousand strings of coins were sent
And silks to the bride with compliment.
Delicacies from land and sea
Were brought by two corteges or three.

Mother Liu told her daughter, "Word
Comes from the governor have you heard?
Tomorrow is your wedding day,
Put yourself in bridal array.
Make your own dress ere it's too late!"
Lanzhi sat in a pensive state.
She sobbed 'neath her handkerchief,

And streaming tears revealed her grief.

She dragged a marble-seated chair,

Towards the window in despair.

In her left hand the scissors bright

And silk and satin in her right.

At noon a jacket new was made

And at dusk a robe in brocade.

Behind dark clouds the sun down crept,

Grief-stricken, she went out and wept.

Zhongqing, at this news of his spouse,

Asks leave and starts out for her house.

After a short ride on his way,

His horse makes an anguished neigh.

This neigh is familiar to her ears;

She comes out before he appears.

She gazes afar, at a loss

What to say when he comes across.

She pats the horse when it comes nigh,

And then says with a woeful sigh,

"Alas! Since you parted with me,

What's happened we could not foresee.

Our hope cannot be realized.

On hearing this, you'll be surprised.

I was compelled by my own mother

Together with my tyrant brother

To wed another man at last.
What can we do? The die is cast."
Jiao Zhongqing tells his former wife,
"I wish you a happier life!
The lofty rock steadfast appears;
It will stand for thousands of years.
Howe'er resistant the vine may be,
'It will lose its toughness easily.
May you live happier day by day!
Alone to death I'll go my way."
"Why say such cruel things to me?"
To her former husband says she,
"We are compelled, both you and I.
How could I live if you should die?
E'en dead, let us together stay!
Forget not what we've said today!"
They stand long hand in hand before
They go each to his or her door.
No lovers know a sharper pain
Than to part till death joins them again.
They're willing to breathe their last breath;
A severed life is worse than death;

Jiao Zhongqing went home full of gloom;
He went straight to his mother's room.

"Today the cold wind blows down trees;
Bitten by frost, the orchids freeze.
Fear my life will end like the tree,
Leaving you alone after me.
That's what such forebodings proclaim.
Don't lay on gods or ghosts the blame!
May you like hillside rock live long.
With your four limbs both straight and strong!"
On hearing this, his mother shed
Copious tears before she said,
"As son of noble family,
A high official you should be.
How could you die for such a wife?
Don't play down on your noble life!
There's a maiden in east neighbourhood,
beside her no one else is good.
I have wooed her to be your spouse;
Soon the reply will come to our house."
Zhongqing retired to his empty room,
determined not to be a bridegroom.
He sighed and glanced towards the hall,
Seeing his tragic curtain fall.

In the blue tent on her wedding day
Lanzhi heard cows, low and steeds neigh.

At dusk the ghostly twilight waned;
The guests gone, lonely she remained.
"My life," she thought, "will end today.
My soul will go, but my body stay."
She doffed her silken shoes to drown
Herself in uprolled wedding gown,
This news came to her Zhongqing's ear;
He would not be severed from his dear.
To and fro in the ward paced he,
Then hanged himself beneath a tree.

Their families, after they died,
Buried them by the mountainside.
Pine trees were planted left and right,
And planes and cypresses on the site.
Their foliage darkens the ground,
Their branches intertwined are found.
A pair of peacocks fly above;
They are well-known as birds of love.
Heads up, they sing song after song,
From night to night, and all night long.
A passer-by would stand spellbound;
A lonely widow would wake dumfound.
Men of posterity, I pray,
Do not forget that bygone day!

NINETEEN OLD POEMS

I

You travel on and on,

Leaving me all alone.

Long miles between us lie

As earth apart from sky.

The road is steep and far;

I can't go where you are.

Northern steeds love cold breeze,

And southern birds warm trees.

The farther you're away;

The thinner I'm each day.

The cloud has veiled the sun;

You won't come back, dear one.

Missing you makes me old;

Soon comes the winter cold.

Alas! Of me you're quit;

I wish you will keep fit.

II

Green, green riverside grass she sees;
Lush, lush the garden's willow trees.
Fair, fair, she waits in painted bower,
Bright, bright like a window-framed flower.
In rosy, rosy dress she stands;
She puts forth slender, slender hands.
A singing girl in early life,
Now she is a deserted wife.
Her husband's gone far, far away.
How to keep lonely bed each day!

III

Green, green, the tombside cypresses are seen;
Clear, clear, the pebbles in the brook appear.
We live between the earth and sky;
Like travelers we shall pass by.
So let's enjoy our cups of wine!
It may not be strong, but it's fine.
Our carriages and steeds let us drive
To the two capitals which thrive!
How splendid is Riverside Town!
The crowned and belted come up and down.

By-streets criss-cross the thoroughfare;
Lordly mansions stand here and there.
Two palaces command far and nigh,
With watch-towers hundred feet high.
Let us enjoy fully our feast!
Why should we worry in the least?

IV

We keep a feast in spirits high;
Our pleasures are hard to relate.
The music played wafts in the sky,
And stirring are songs up-to-date.
The virtuosoes sing their fill;
The connoisseurs know what's about.
At heart they all have the same will,
But none of them will speak it out.
Men live like rovers on their way
Or dust by wind driven away.
Why don't you ride at a fast pace
And occupy important place?
Why should one live in poverty
And suffer life-long misery!

V

In northwest there's a tower proud;
It stands as high as floating cloud.
Its curtained lattice window flares
Between the eaves and flights of stairs.
Music from there comes to my ear,
Its sound so sad, its tune so drear.
Who could compose such doeful song
But one whose secret grief's life-long?
Sad music rises with the breeze;
The middle tune wafts ill at ease.
It's followed then by three refrains;
At last indignant, it complains.
For the musician out of view,
I sigh that connoisseurs are few.
I would become a crane to sing
With her while flying wing to wing.

VI

I gather lotus blooms across the stream
In orchid marsh where fragrant flowers teem.
To whom shall I send what I pluck today?
The one I love is living far away.
I turn my eyes towards our old abode.
O what can I find but a long, long road.
Living apart, how can we be consoled?
Our hearts are one,
I'll grieve till I grow old.

VII

The moon shines bright at dead of night;
The crickets chirp by eastern wall.
The Plough's bar points to winter white;
Stars can be counted one and all.
Wild grass wet with dew far and nigh,
How fast seasons change and come back!
Among the trees cicadas cry.
Where are south-flying swallows black?
Now I remember my compeers
Soaring on high into the cloud.
Forgetting friends of bygone years,
They leave me like trace of the crowd.

The Northern and Southern stars mock
At Winnow Star which sifts no grain.
No friendship is as firm as rock.
What's the use to have names in vain!

VIII

Frail, frail the lonely bamboo's root
Clinging to lofty mountain's foot,
I'm newly wed to husband mine
Like dodder clinging to the vine.
The dodder has its time to grow;
A couple should together go.
But thousand-mile mountains divide
The newly-wed one on each side.
Longing for him makes me grow old.
Why won't his cab come to household?
I grieve for orchid flower white;
Petals unfurled, it looks so bright.
If it's not plucked in blossom time,
It fades with grass after its prime.
In his consistence I believe.
What can I do? Why should I grieve?

IX

A rare tree stands in courtyard quiet;
Among green leaves flowers run riot.
I bend a branch and pluck its bloom
To send to my far-off dear groom.
Its fragrance fills my breast and sleeves
Unsent so far away, it grieves.
I value not the bloom sweet-hearted,
But I am grieved so long we've parted.

X

Far, far away the Cowherd Star;
Bright, bright riverside Weaving Maid.
Slender, slender her fingers are;
Clack, clack her shuttle's tune is played.
She weaves all day, no web is done;
Like rain her tears drop one by one.
Heaven's River's shallow and clear;
The two stars are not far apart,
Where brimful, brimful waves appear,
They gaze but can't lay bare their heart.

XI

I turn my carriage and set out;
Along an endless road I pass.
I see a wilderness about;
The eastern wind shakes grass on grass.
I meet with nothing old at all.
Can I not olden nevertheless?
Every thing has its rise and fall.
Do not delay to win success!
Man is not made of metal or stones.
Can we live to hundred years old?
We'll soon become a heap of bones.
Let's value glory more than gold!

XII

The eastern wall stands long and high;
It girds the town from end to end.
The autumn wind sweeps far and nigh;
The withered grass and green grass bend.
How fast the seasons change and part!
How soon comes the end of the year!
The pheasants cry with bitter heart;
The crickets' chirp would hasten tears.
Wash grief away from its deep root!
Why should you bind your hand and foot!
In northern land are beauties we desire;
The fairest has a face as fine as jade.
Behold! she is dressed in silken attire;
Listen! before the window music's played.
Why is the melody so sad and drear?
The peg has tightened and quickened the string,
Amorous, with loose girdle she comes near;
But she still hesitates while loitering.
"Could we be a pair of swallows in flight,
I would peck clods in your nest with delight."

XIII

I drive my car through Upper Eastern Gate,
And see from afar the Northern Tomb.
How poplar leaves rustle and agitate!
Pines and cypresses flank the way with gloom.
Beneath lie those who died long, long ago;
Buried in eternal darkness they remain.
They sleep beside the Yellow Springs below;
From year to year they never wake again.
How many days and nights have come and passed!
The years we'ro given fleet like morning dew.
Life is a journey which can never last
As long as stone or meta! old and new.
Do you want to enjoy longevity?
But in the end even saints and sages die.
If you by drugs seek immortality,
There's no elixir on which to rely.
Better to drink wine whenever you may,
And dress in silk and satin everyday!

XIV

The bygone times are gone farther away;

The forthcoming becomes dearer each day.

I go out of the gate and strain my eye;

I only see mounds and tombs far and nigh.

The ancient graveyards into fields are ploughed;

Firewood is made of pine and cypress proud.

White poplars give out their heart-breaking breath;

To hear their sigh on sigh I'm grieved to death.

I wish to go back to my dear abode.

But how can I traverse the long, long road!

XV

Few live as long as a hundred years.

Why grieve over a thousand in tears!

When days grows short and long grows night,

Why not go out in candlelight?

Enjoy the present time in laughter!

Why worry about the hereafter?

If you won't spend the wealth you've got,

Posterity would call you sot.

We cannot hope to rise as high

As an immortal in the sky.

XVI

Cold, cold the end of year draws near;
Crickets at night chirp sad and drear.
The piercing wind blows up and down;
Abroad, you have no winter gown.
At home your broidered quilt is left;
Why of my mate am I bereft?
Lonely I stay through the long night.
Can I not dream of your face bright?
Can you forget our wedding day;
You gave me reins on homeward way?
I wish we'd live long side by side,
Come back hand in hand in our ride.
You came in dream not for an hour,
Nor would you stay long in my bower.
Awake, I have no wings to fly.
How can I rise with the wind high?
I try to please you from afar,
And crane my neck toward where you are.
Leaning at the gate, I deplore;
My tears fall and moisten the door.

XVII

In early winter the cold air comes forth.

How sharp is the biting wind from the north!

Sorrowful, I know how long is the night;

Looking up, I count the stars teeming bright.

On the fifteenth day full waxes the moon;

But on the twentieth it will wane so soon.

A traveler coming from far away

Gives me a letter which begins to say

My far-off husband longs for his dear wife,

And ends by an adieu as long as life.

I put this letter in my inner vest:

For three years no word has dimmed in my breast.

I cherish with whole heart each word, each dot,

But I'm afraid my husband knows it not.

XVIII

A guest who came from afar said
He'd brought me a roll of brocade.
From my husband I'm far apart;
This roll of brocade shows his heart.
Broidered with lovebirds in silk thread,
I'll make a quilt for lovers' bed,
Filled with floss not to be forgot
And fringed with tight knot on knot.
Like lacquer melted in the glue,
Let's be inseparably true!

XIX

How bright are moonbeams shed
On my silk-curtained bed!
I cannot sleep, so sad;
I pace up and down, clad.
One may find joy abroad,
But less than in his abode.
I stroll outdoors alone.
To whom make my grief known?
I crane my neck in vain;
Come in, tears fall like rain.

THE OLD WIFE AND THE NEW

She went uphill to pluck herbs wild;
Downhill, she met her former husband mild.
She knelt and asked, "How do you...
How do you find your young wife new?"
"Though my new wife is good and fair,
She cannot yet with you compare.
In looks by your side she may stand
But she's less clever with her hand.
When she came in from the front door,
You left your room on second floor.
She's good at embroidering skein,
While you are good at sewing plain.
She weaves one foot of silk a day;
You weave five feet without delay.
Her works compared with yours, all told!
The new is not up to the old."

I STROLL OUT OF THE EAST GATE

I stroll out of the east gate of the town;
On the road to southern shore I look down.
In wind and snow the day before yesterday
Along this road my friend did go away.
I'd follow him and go across the stream,
But water's deep and there's no bridge nor beam.
If like two yellow birds we'd soar up high,
Then homeward to our native land we'd fly.

HOMECOMING AFTER WAR

At fifteen I left home to fight the foe
And cannot come back till I am fourscore.
On the way I meet a countryman I know;
I ask him who remains within my door.
"Seen from afar, your house is over there,"
"Mid graves where pine and cypress stand aloof."
Arrived, I see in dog hole run a hare
And pheasants fly from the beam of my roof.
In middle courtyard grows only wild grain
And by the well grows mallow I can eat.
I pluck the grain and boil it as food plain
And put the mallow in the soup I heat.
When I have cooked the simple, homely fare,
Who will eat it with me? No one appears.
I go outdoors and eastwards fix my stare,
My furrowed face and clothes wet with tears.

Cai Yan (c. 200)

THE LAMENTATIONS

Han's power in decay,
Premier Dong Zhuo held sway.
He would usurp the throne,
Ministers' lives laid down.
Moving the capital,
He rose on Empire's fall.
Revolting armies rose
And gave the premier blows.
Dong's Tartars came to fight
In golden armour bright.
Revolters were not strong
Against Tartars' spears long.
They lost the besieged town;
The revolt was put down.
Revolters were all slain,
Unburied on the plain.
Their heads hung from horse's side
While women captives cried,
Driven through the West Pass
On tortuous way, alas!
Looking back far away,
Heart-broken, what to say!

Ten thousand men, all told,
Were captured, young and old.
Among kinsmen or brothers
None dared to speak to others.
Angry soldiers would shout
To kill captives about.
They brandished swords to kill
Those who revolted still.
For our lives could we care?
Insults were hard to bear.
Beaten now and again,
How could we bear the pain!
We marched all the way
And wailed all night and day.
We could nor live nor die,
And knew not how or why.
How much have we done wrong
As to suffer so long!

People on border land
Work hard from hand to hand.
Their fields covered with snow,
Cold wind in spring will blow.

My heart would freeze to hear
It wrinkled face and ear.
Thinking of parents dear,
I sighed with grief and fear.
When visitors came here,
We welcomed them with cheer.
They brought no news from home,
Which belied our welcome.
How lucky I was then
Ransomed by my kinsmen!
Released, I had to leave
My sons. How it would grieve
A loving mother's heart
With her dear sons to part
And not to reunite,
Live or die, day and night!
They came to my embrace
And asked about the place
Where I would go and when
I would come back again.
How could a mother kind
Leave her children behind?

Grown up they were not yet,

Whom I should not forget.

In tears, with broken heart,

How could I from them part!

Caressing them with hand,

I could not start but stand.

The countrymen I knew

Came to bid me adieu.

My return made them glad,

But at heart they felt sad.

The steeds stamped on the ground,

Cab wheels would not turn round.

This moved the passers-by,

Who would not go but sigh.

My sons far, far away,

I longed for them each day.

Between us long, long miles,

When could I see their smiles?

They were sons I had born,

Could I not be care-worn?

Back home, I looked about,

None within or without.

Walls turned to woody mounds,
Thorns grew over the grounds.
Bleak bones unburied lay,
Uncovered all the way.
Outdoors no human word
But howling wolves were heard.
Facing my shadow only,
Heart-broken, I felt lonely.
Gazing far from the height,
I felt my soul in flight.
My life seems to end,
If not saved by a friend.
Forced to breathe a hard breath,
My life is hard as death.
So I entrust my fate
To the new friendly mate.
Not honored as before,
I've a life to deplore.
It will soon pass away.
When will come my last day?

Cao Cao[①](155–220)

GRAVEYARD SONG

East of the Pass there're heroes brave and bright,

They rose in arms against the worst man of all.

They formed alliance first on River's right

And joined their force to take the capital.

But they were not united with might and main,

So like wild geese they straggled all about.

They fought each other for power or gain,

And tried to kill each other and fell out.

The self-styled monarch rules the southern shore;

The royal seal is carved on northern land.

Men long in arms grow lousy more and more;

Countless people die when they cannot stand.

Afield lie bones of those who lost their lives;

For miles and miles no cock is heard to crow.

Among a hundred people one survives;

My heart would break on thinking of the woe.

---

① King of the State of Wei, one of the Three Kingdoms (220–280).

A SHORT SONG

We should sing before wine.
For how long can life last?
Like dew on morning fine,
So many days have passed.
How can we be unbound
By grief which weighed us down?
Grief can only be drowned
In wine of good renown.
Talents with collars blue,
For you I pine away.
So much I long for you,
My heart aches night and day.
How gaily call the deer
While grazing in the shade!
When I have talents here,
Let lute and lyre be played!
Bright as the moon on high,
How can I bring it down?
Grief from within comes nigh;
Ceaselessly it flows on.
Across the fields and lanes,
You are kind to come here.

Talking of far-off plains,

You cherish friendship dear.

The moon's bright and stars nice,

The crows in southward flight

They circle the trees thrice;

There's no branch to alight.

With crags high mountains rise;

With water the sea's deep.

With the help of the wise,

An ordered world we'll keep.

SONG OF THE COLD ENDURED

Northward we go up mountains stiff.

How hard it is to climb the cliff!

The footpath twists like gut of sheep;

The cartwheels break against crags steep.

The trembling trees are stark and bleak;

The northern wind moans on the peak.

Before us crouch bears brown and black;

Tigers and leopards howl by the track.

In these vals few people have passed,
And snow is falling thick and fast.
I stretch my neck with long, long sigh;
The hard campaign to grief gives rise.
Why has grief in my heart increased?
All I want is to go back east.
There is no bridge on water deep;
We know not how o'er it to sweep.
And halfway up, we go astray;
At dusk we find nowhere to stay.
Each day go farther off our forces;
Our men are hungry as their horses.
Pack on shoulder, we snatch firewood
And chop ice to boil as our food.
Of Eastern Hills the soldiers' song[1]
Saddens my heart and soul for long.

---

[1] The song sung by the soldiers of the Duke of Zhou when they had put
down a rebellion in the Eastern Hills after 1125 BC.

THE SEA

I come to view the boundless ocean

From Stony Hill on eastern shore.

Its water rolls in rhythmic motion

And islands stand amid its roar.

Tree on tree grows from peak to peak;

Grass on grass looks lush far and nigh.

The autumn wind blows drear and bleak

The monstrous billows surge up high.

The sun by day, the moon by night

Appear to rise up from the deep.

The Milky Way with stars so bright

Sinks down into the sea in sleep.

How happy I feel at this sight!

I croon this poem in delight.

INDOMITABLE SOUL

Although long lives the tortoise wise,
In the end he cannot but die.
The serpent in the mist may rise,
But in the dust he too shall lie.
Although the stabled steed is old,
He dreams to run for mile and mile.
In life's December heroes bold
Won't change indomitable style.
It's not up to Heaven alone
To lengthen or shorten our day.
To a great age we can live on,
If we keep fit, cheerful and gay.
How happy I feel at this thought!
I croon this poem as I ought.

Wang Can (177–217)

SEVEN SORROWS

I

The Western Capital in woe:

Nowhere but wolves and tigers go.

I leave the central land again,

And go off to southern plain.

Facing me, kin and parents grieve;

Following me, friends will not leave.

What do I see out city gate?

White bones strew the plain desolate,

A starving woman cannot feed

Her child and lays it in the weed.

She looks back at its wailing sound,

And goes in tears, not turning round.

"I know not how long I'll survive.

Can I keep both of us alive?"

I whip my horse and leave them there;

To hear such words I cannot bear.

I go south on Royal Tomb's crest,

And gaze back on Capital West.

How could a patriot from it part?

I heave a sigh with broken heart.

SEVEN SORROWS

II

Homeless am I on Southern Plain,
How should I here so long remain?
Twin boats sail side by side upstream;
The setting sun grieves me in dream.
On mountain ridges sinks afterglow,
In rocky vales shadows o'erflow.
Foxes run to their den for rest,
Birds hover over their old nest.
I seem to hear the ripples ring;
By riverside the monkeys sing.
A fleet breeze blows against my sleeves;
My lapel wet with white dew grieves.
I cannot sleep when night is mute,
I don my robe and play my lute.
Strings seem to sympathize with me,
When vibrates their sad melody.
A roamer's heart so full of care,
My homesickness is hard to bear.

JOINING THE ARMY

Far, far away our army goes
To punish our Southeastern foes,
On the broad stream sails boat on boat;
In twilight boats are still afloat.
The sun half sinks behind west hill;
There's afterglow in homeland still.
The crickets sing by riverside,
A lonely bird flies far and wide,
Warriors are care-worn for their part;
Homesickness has saddened my heart.
I leave my boat to mount a height,
The dew-wet grass moistens my sight.
Turning back, I go to bedside.
To whom can I my grief confide?
The spear and shield require my care.
Should I think of private affair?
We are ordered to win the war.
What to do but go on before?

Chen Lin (?–217)

I WATER MY STEED

I water steed at the foot of Great Wall;

The water in the cave is piercing cold.

I go to see the man in charge of all:

"Do not keep us from home till we grow old!"

"The public works have their table of time.

Go and swing your hammer and sing in chime!"

"A man would rather die in battlefield

Than toil at the Wall with hammer to wield."

The Wall is serpentine and long;

It stretches out three thousand miles.

How many men on border are strong!

Their wives at home stay without smiles.

I send a letter to my wife:

"Remarry and lead a new life!

Serve well your mother-in-law new,

But do not keep your former husband out of view!"

Her letter in reply comes to the border:

"How can your mind be in such a disorder?

Now that you are in woe,

Could I leave you and elsewhere go?"

"If sons are born, put them aside!

If daughters, feed them with meat dried!

Do you not see by the Great Wall

Sons become a heap of bones one and all?"

"I've served you since I bound up my hair,

And constant for you is my care.

I know your grief in borderland.

But if alone, can I long stand?"

Liu Zhen (?–217)

THE PINE—TO MY COUSIN

The pine on hill-top towers high;

The winds in the val sough and sigh.

However violent they may be,

Unshakable stands the pine-tree.

The ice and forest look sad and drear;

The tree stands straight throughout the year.

Does it not fear the biting cold?

It stands on its own as of old.

Xu Gan (171–217)

A Wife's Thoughts

The floating cloud is like an ocean.
Will it convey my heart's emotion?
On wafting cloud I can't rely;
I pace up and down with a sigh.
Men part but they will meet again.
Why lonely should I e'er remain?
Since you left me and went away,
My mirror's dusted with each day.
My thoughts of you like river flow,
O when can they no longer grow?

Po Qin (?–218)

A WOMAN'S LOVE

I went out of the eastern gate,

And met by chance a handsome mate.

To a sweet bower I was led;

Undressed, I served him in the bed.

We did not date 'neath mulberry;

By the roadside our love was free.

I was enchanted at his sight,

My beauty gave him sweet delight.

How to express our loving heart?

Two golden bracelets for my part.

How to express his gallantry?

Two silver rings were given to me.

How to express our feeling dear?

Two bright pearls hanging from the ear.

How to express feelings we nurse?

Behind the elbow a perfume purse.

How to express love in our tryst?

Two jade bracelets around the wrist.

How could I know our love won't fade?

Silken girdles adorned with jade.

How could I know our hearts unite?

Two needles joined by a thread white.

How could I know deep love within?
My hair adorned with gold-foiled pin.
How to console our parting drear?
The turtle pin behind the ear.
How to remember our delight?
A silken robe with three fringes white.
How to express the grief I bear.
The white silk vest and underwear.
How to forget old sorrow sweet?
Far-going shoes upon his feet.
Where did he have with me a date?
East of the mountain did I wait.
At dusk, oh! he did not come down,
But the east wind ruffled my gown.
I looked far, none did appear;
At a loss, I shed tear on tear.
Where did he have with me a date?
South of the mountain did I wait.
At noon, oh! he came not with zest,
But the south wind ruffled my vest.
I could not see him, far apart;
Waiting for him would break my heart.

When did he have with me a date?
West of the mountain did I wait.
At sunset he did not come by;
I loitered and heaved a long sigh.
Looking far, I felt the wind cold.
And up and down my robe was rolled.
Where did he have with me a date?
North of the mountain did I wait.
At nightfall he did not appear;
My dress was ruffled by wind drear.
Longing for him, I could not sit;
My heart broken, could I keep fit?
Why had he loved my person fair?
For youth and beauty he did care.
Had his heart felt love for his mate,
No doubt would he then keep his date.
Lifting my robe! I tread thick grass,
Thinking he'd not deceive, alas!
I turn and loiter high and low;
My poor heart knows not where to go.
I'm grieved to find my love has fled;
My tears stream down like silken thread.

Cao Pi[①] (187–226)

SONG OF A LONELY WIFE

The weather turns cold when bleak blows the autumn breeze;

The leaves shiver and fall into frost dew-drops freeze;

Swallows in group fly south together with wild geese.

I miss you far apart till broken is my heart.

A traveler may roam but he'll yearn for his home.

Why so long should you stay in a land far away?

I remain sad and lonely in empty chamber only.

Though grieved, I dare not my dear lord to forget, yet

I do not know my gown wet with tears streaming down.

I take my lute and ring its melancholy string.

I sing low a short song. Oh how can it be long?

The bright moon overhead sheds its light on my bed.

The River of Stars peep westward when night is deep.

The Cowherd from afar gazes on Weaving Star,

What is wrong on their part to be kept far apart!

---

① Eldest son of Cao Cao and emperor of Wei (reigned 220–226).

THE LOTUS POND

We ride in royal carriage light,
And stroll in west garden at night.
Two canals along the park gleam,
Leafy trees cast shade on the stream.
Branches stroke our canopy high,
Longer ones seem to scrape the sky
A sudden gale hastens our wheels,
A bird flying before us reels.
See rosy beams the bright moon sprinkles
And bloomlike clouds star on star wrinkles.
Heaven sheds brilliance from above
And dazzling hues for us to love.
As immortals we are not strong,
How could we lead a life as long?
Let us be free to roam at will,
And of our life enjoy our fill!

NOSTALGIA

Long, long the autumn night,
Chill, chill the north winds bite.
I cannot sleep but toss,
Don and rise at a loss.
My gown is wet with dew,
I'm lost in thoughts anew.

Below I see waves clear;
Above the moon seems near.
The Milky Way afar
Criss-cross with star on star.
Insects sing mournful plight,
Wild geese in lonely flight.
Sad, sad thoughts assail me;
Long, long I can't be free.
Could I have wings and beam
Or bridge to cross the stream?
I sigh to the west breeze;
My heart sinks ill at ease.

A ROAMER'S SONG

In northwest clouds float by
Just like pavilions high.
I am unfortunate
To wander is my fate.
Blown on the southeast way,
In Kingdom Wu I'd stay.
Wu is not my homeland.
How could I there long stand?
Leave it and speak no more!
Could I like foreign shore?

Cao Zhi[1] (192–232)

OH, TUMBLEWEED

Oh, tumbleweed roaming afar!
How lonely in the world you are!
From your root you roam far away,
Without any rest night and day,
East and west over nine or seven
North and south fields under the heaven.
See a whirlwind suddenly rise
And blow you into cloudy skies.
Expecting to go heavenly way,
Suddenly in abyss you stay.
A startling whirlwind pulls you out
Back to Mid-Field or thereabout.
You will go south, but it turns north;
When east you go, west it blows forth.
Helpless, on whom can you depend?
Your life seems to come to an end.
Across eight lakes you have been swept;
Over five mountains you have leapt.
You roam and ramble in distress.
Oh, but who knows your bitterness?

---

[1] Younger brother of Cao Pi.

Better to be a blade of grass
To be burned by wild fire, alas!
You know, of course, death will cause pain.
What joy to join your root again!

SONG OF THE HARP

Good wine is served in palace high;
Friends are invited from far and nigh.
Cooks have prepared a sumptuous feast;
They've killed fat sheep, cattle and beast.
The western lutes play lofty strains;
The eastern, harmonious refrains.
Ladies like swallows dance along;
Fair songstresses sing their best song.
After passing three rounds of wine,
We loosen our belts for dish fine.
The host offers pieces of gold;
The guests wish him to live till old,
Not to forget friendship lasts long,
And injustice can't but be wrong.

Modesty's what good men adore.

What do we, bowing, need for more?

Surprised the wind blows off the sun,

Westward we see the day has done.

Could we see splendid times again?

A hundred years will pass amain.

Today we live in capital,

Which would soon turn to ruined hall.

There were no ancient sages but died;

Knowing our destiny, we sighed.

An Oriole in the Field

The grievous wind raves through tall trees
And raises billows on the seas.
Without a sharpened sword in hand,
In vain have I friends in the land.
Have you not seen an oriole fall
In trap on hearing a hawk's call?
The fowler's glad to trap the bird.
Could I stand by without a word?
I cut the net to set it free
So that from the trap it may flee.
It flies up to the azure sky
And down to thank the stander-by.

Song of the Capital

Ladies in capital are full of charms,
And gallant young men are skilful at arms.
My sword is worth its weight in gold, no less
Is worth my fashionable riding dress.
On eastern pathway I would watch cocks fight;
I run my steed between the poplars white.

I gallop when halfway I've not yet done;

I see before my horse two rabbits run.

Armed with my whistling arrows and long bow,

To the southern mountain swiftly I go.

My left hand holds the bow for my right to shoot,

At one blow two rabbits killed at my foot.

My skill not fully displayed, down I bring,

On looking up, an eagle on the wing.

All the spectators say I'm a good shot;

To my archery's attributed a lot.

Come back, we feast in western hall and ask

For wine which costs ten thousand coins a cask.

We have rich soup of carp and braised shrimp meat,

Delicious turtle and bear's paw to eat.

Friends are invited to take their seats among

Poets and songstresses at a table long.

We beat at the musical earthernware

In different ways, deftly here and there.

The sun runs fast and sinks in the southwest;

Thus time and tide will not wait for our guest.

Like cloud we scatter while bidding adieu;

Tomorrow morning here we'll meet anew.

Song of a Beauty

A maiden fair is full of charm and grace;
She gathers mulberry leaves at crisscross place.
The tender branches rustle one and all;
How many mulberry leaves moan and fall!
Her arms so white are seen with sleeves uprolled;
Around her wrist a bracelet made of gold.
A golden sparrow pin adorns her hair;
A green jade pendant hangs at her waist fair.
Her lovely form encompassed with pearls bright
And carol and blue glass beads left and right.
How do her silken dresses flow with ease
And her light skirt flutter with gentle breeze!
Her melting glance reveals her shining eye;
In her sweet breath you hear the orchid sigh.
The travelers en route would halt their car;
Those resting would forget where their meals are.
If you ask where is her house of renown,
It stands at the southern end of the town.
Her house by the highway has floor on floor;
It's green with a high gate and double door.
She looks as radiant as the morning sun.
Who'd not admire such a beautiful one?

Why are the busy go-between delayed?

Where are betrothal gifts of silk and jade?

The maiden fair longs for a worthy mate;

It's hard to find one, so she has to wait.

People in vain may gossip a great deal.

What do they know of her lofty ideal?

She lives alone at her prime, fair and bright.

How can she not sigh at the dead of night!

SONG OF THE WHITE HORSE

A white horse gallops in its golden gear

As if in flight to north western frontier.

Who is the cavalier in hurry great?

A gallant hero of the northern state.

While he was young, he left his native land;

His name was known as far as border sand.

Since then he's learned to draw the strongest bow

And shoot arrows of hard wood high and low.

He bends the string and hits the target at left,

And at destroying that at right he's deft.

Looking up, he shoots a bird fast in speed;
Bowing down, he breaks the hoof of a steed.
To be more swift than gibbons is not hard,
Nor to be strong and daring like a pard.
The border towns along northwest frontiers
Are oft invaded by Hunnish cavaliers.
When urgent messages come from northern side,
At once to the high fortress he would ride.
Straightforward he would drive against the Huns;
Turning back, he would beat Tartarian sons.
At the point of the sword in the hard strife,
How could he care for individual life?
He'd take no heed of his father and mother,
Let alone wife, children or any other.
Of heroes brave his name is on the roll;
He would not care when his death knell would toll.
The state at stake, he would give his last breath.
Would a homegoing soul fear to face death?

SONG TO THE PRINCE OF WHITE HORSE[①]

After the audience in the Brilliance Hall

Then each of us returns to his domain.

At dawn we leave the royal capital;

At dusk the hill where brothers starved with pain.

The Rivers Yi and Luo are wide and deep,

And there's no bridge across the two streams broad.

Over giant billows our boats bob and leap,

And we complain of long, long eastern road.

Looking back, from the city gate we part;

I crane my neck while sorrow gnaws my heart.

How vast and wild the valley great!

The shades of trees darken green hills.

Rain's muddied my way desolate;

Crisscross the swollen water spills.

The road breaks midway, overflowed;

---

① Half brother of Cao Zhi, persecuted both by their eldest brother Cao
  Pi, emperor of Wei (reigned 220–226).

I veer and drive up mountains high.
An endless slope climbs to the cloud;
My tired horse feels dizzy and shy.

Dizzy, my horse can still go on;
Gloomy, my thoughts are sad and drear.
Sad and drear, what to think upon?
Far, far apart those dear and near.
We would together forward go;
Midway we have to separate.
At capital screech owl and crow;
jackals and wolves bar royal gate.
Blue flies would turn white into black;
Between kinsmen slanderers stand.
There's no way for me to go back;
I am at a loss, reins in hand.

Though at a loss, how can I stay?
I'll think of you till we grow old.
The autumn wind brings chilly day;
By my side chirp cicadas cold.
How wilderness is bare and bleak!
The sun is soon lost in the west.
For the tall trees homing birds seek,
Flapping their wings towards their nest.

A lonely beast seeks its counterpart;
Grass in its jaws, when can it eat?
At their sight I feel sad at heart;
Deeply I sigh to slow its beat.

Deeply I sigh: What can I do?
I can't oppose High Heaven's will.
My brother[1] born by my mother too,
Dead, cannot come over val and hill.
His lonely soul haunts his old place;
In capital his coffin stays.
The living pass away apace;
The dead will soon sink in decays.
In a short life a man appears,
And disappears like morning dew.
We'll come to the end of our years
Like shadows we cannot pursue.
I'm not made of metal or stone.
How can I not be grieved alone!

I'm grieved, my spirit ill at ease.

---

[1] Younger brother of Cao Zhi, poisoned by Cao Pi.

Lay it aside and say no more!
A brave man aims at the four seas,
A thousand miles near as next door.
If love and bounty are well fed,
Distance cannot keep us apart.
Why should we share the quilt in bed
Before we can lay bare our heart?
If we are grieved as to fall sick,
Like women tears would fall in rain.
Our parting moves me to the quick.
Can I not brood with bitter pain?

What do I think of bitter pain?
Heaven's decree can't be believed.
I seek immortals but in vain;
By them I have long been deceived.
Change will come in a moment fleet.
Who can live to a hundred years old?
We part perhaps never to meet.
Who'll clasp again your hand I hold?
Prince, take care of your body dear!
Let us enjoy old age in view!
I take my road and wipe my tears;
I write these lines as our adieu.

PARTING WITH YING AT LUOYANG^①

We climb on foot up Northern Hill
And gaze from far on Luoyang town.
The ruined capital looks still;
All the palaces were burned down.
Walls and fence rows gaping and torn,
Brambles and thorns spread to the sky.
No more old men in dress out-worn,
All we meet are young passers-by.
We cannot sidle the pathway;
The wilderness will nothing yield.
If far away you long did stay,
You could not find the path afield.
How bleak and bare the Central Plain!
No cooking fires for miles around.
Thinking of our former domain,
My breath chokes up, I am dumb found.

---

① The Luoyang palaces had been burned in 190 by Dong Zhuo and the
city suffered terribly in the civil war that ensued.

SEVEN POEMS
IV

A beauty lives in southern lands[1];
As fair as peach in bloom she stands.
At dawn she wanders left and right
Of Rivers Xiao and Xiang till night.
For rosy face the world won't care.
Who would praise her teeth bright and fair?
She sinks or swims, time flies so fast.
Alas! how could her prime long last!

---

[1] Cao Zhi, persecuted by his eldest brother Cao Pi, compares himself to a beauty unsuited for.

LAMENT

Streams of light on the tower softly play;

It seems the moon is loath to move away.

For here is beauty wilting, tender sighs

Telling of tender heart in pain, which cries.

May we ask who is there so full of ruth?

A wife in name, a widow, ah! in truth.

"You are far, far away for over ten years;

I am alone, alone and oft in tears.

You're like the dust drawn upward on the way;

Like mud in dirty water still I stay.

One sinking, the other swimming we remain.

If ever, when are we to meet again?

Would that I were the wind from the southwest

That I could rush across the land to your breast!

If you from your embrace should shut me out,

Where could I go? Where should I roam about?"

WRITTEN WHILE TAKING SEVEN PACES^①

Pods burned to cook peas;
Peas weep in the pot:
"Grown from the same trees,
Why boil us so hot?"

---

① The poet won the favor of his father for his literary talent and lost that of his eldest brother, who later became the first emperor of Wei and ordered him, under pain of death, to compose this poem within the time of taking seven paces.

Ji Kang (223–262)

To My Brother Giving up the Pen for the Sword
IX

On steed you go, In dress so bright.
At left a bow, Arrows at right.
You shoot birds fast In flight like breeze.
On plains you've passed, Gazing with ease.

Ruan Ji (210–263)

Reflections
I

I cannot sleep deep in the night;
I rise and sit to play my lute.
Thin curtains mirror the moon bright;
Clear breezes tug my lapels mute.
A lonely swan shrieks over the plain;
Hovering birds cry in north wood.
What do I see, pacing in vain?
My heart is grieved in solitude.

III

The eastern garden's trodden way
Leads to blooming peach and plum trees.
But withered leaves are blown away
And drifting in the autumn breeze.
Bright flowers languish soon and fade;
With thorns the hall will be overgrown.
Leave the hall on horse and evade
To Hermits' hill and settle down!
Hard to keep you from being lost,
Let alone your children and wife.
Wild grass will be covered with frost;
Soon will end the year and our life.

Fu Xuan (218–278)

THE CARRIAGES ROLL

The carriages roll, oh! the horses run;
I think of you, oh! my dearest one!
Where are you now? oh! you're out of view.
Like your shadow, oh! I'd follow you.
It disappears, oh! when you're in shade;
You're in the sun, oh! and it won't fade.

Zhang Hua (232–300)

LOVE POEMS

III

The soft breeze ripples curtains drawn
In lonely moonlit room at dawn.
My love still stays in far-off place;
My orchid room sees not his face.
In vain I embrace moonlight shed
On the thin quilt over empty bed.
I regret happy days in flight;
I complain of long, long sad night.
Tapping my pillow, deep I sigh;
With broken heart I cannot cry.

V

I freely gaze on countryside;
Alone I linger in the gloom.
Sweet orchids grow along streams wide;
Green islets shaded by trees in bloom.
But my beloved one is not here;
I gather these flowers in vain.
Birds in the nest know the wind drear;
Ants in the cave the drenching rain.
If you have not been far apart,
How can you value your sweetheart?

Pan Yue (247–300)

ELEGY ON MY WIFE

Winter and spring slip by;
Cold weather turns to heat.
In grave her remains lie;
We're severed never to meet.

Can I do what I will?
What use to linger here?
Better return to fill
My post of former year.
Seeing our house and room,
I think of her in vain.
Her shadow lost in gloom,
Her writings still remain.
Her perfume in the air,
Her portrait on the wall,
She seems alive still there;
I'm startled beyond call.
Like single bird on high
Whose mate was lost one day;
Like flatfish with one eye,
The other blind midway.
Spring wind brings no delight;
Morning dew drips from eaves.
I dream of her by night;
Day on day piled up grieves.
When won't my sorrow rise?
I'd play the lute like the wise.

Shi Chong[1] (249–300)

SONG OF THE BRIGHT LADY

I am a daughter of the Han,

But wedded to the Tartar Khan.

I'd hardly finished my goodbye

When forerunners held banners high.

The servants wept to leave their home;

Carriage steeds neighed with mouth in foam.

With sorrow my heart broke and bled;

Tears fell and wet my ribbons red.

We went far and farther away

And reached the Tartar town one day.

Ushered into the Dome of fame,

I was called Queen Yanzhi by name.

In foreign tribe I'm ill at ease;

The high position does not please.

Wed first to father, then to son,

Surprise and shame would not be done.

To be or not to be in strife,

Silent, I lead ignoble life.

---

[1] The richest man of the Jin Dynasty, who wrote in the first person about the lady wed to the Tartar Khan in 33 B. C.

Ignoble life without relief,

My heart is filled with wrath and grief.

I'd ride on the wings of wild geese

To fly far away where I please.

But the wild geese don't care for me

I stand long in anxiety.

I was a jade people admire;

I'm now a flower in the mire.

The flower falls at dusk, alas!

I'd be withered with autumn grass.

To my posterity I'd say:

Hard fate to be wed far away!

Lu Ji (261–303)

ON MY WAY TO LUOYANG

I go far across hill and rill;
Mountains and streams stretch far and wide.
I whip my horse to climb the hill;
I rein up along countryside.
Hugging my shadow, I sleep at night;
Startling at dawn, I'm ill at ease.
I lean on rocks while I alight,
I lend my ears to mournful breeze.
Clear dewdrops drip when night is deep.
How brilliant is the full, round moon!
Hugging my pillow, I can't sleep;
Shaking dust off, I muse alone.

Zuo Si(250–305)

ON HISTORY

I

At twenty I could write;

All books on me shed light.

I'd discuss state affair

And build castles in air.

The foe invaded our border;

Here came urgency order.

Though no armor I wore,

I learned the art of war.

I'd croon to stir winds clear

To quell the east frontier.

A dull sword could cut still;

My dream is hard to fill.

I'd see on either side

South and West pacified.

No post shall be my lot;

I'd return to my cot.

II

Gloomy the pine in valley deep;

Lush is the grass on mountain steep.

The latter's only one inch long;

But higher than the former strong.

The noble in position high,

The able in low office sigh.

In different places they stay;

Their places are not built in a day.

Jin and Zhang were families old;[1]

They had served seven reigns, all told.

Not that white-haired Feng was not great,

But low was royal estimate.

---

[1] This is a satire against the nobles in high position (Jin and Zhang) while the able (Feng) was in low office.

Zhang Han

THINKING OF THE EASTERN STREAM

The rise of autumn breeze, oh!

Makes leaves fall from the trees.

Water of Eastern Stream, oh!

Has fattened perch and bream.

I'm miles and miles away; oh!

When's my home-going day?

How can I not heave sighs, oh!

My face turned to the skies!

Zhang Zai

SONG OF SEVEN SORROWS

Graves pile on graves on northern hill;

Three or five tombs are higher still.

Who lie in the tombs of the three?

Emperors of Han dynasty.

Imperial tombs stand face to face;

Overgrown with weeds is now the place.

When turmoil rose, the times were hard;

Robbers came like tiger or pard.

Graveyard was destroyed far and wide,
Tombs opened in the countryside.
The corpse deprived of jewel boxes,
The robbers plundered them like foxes.
In ruins lie the temple halls
And crumbled the enclosing walls.
In dim light thorns and brambles grow;
On footpath herds and cowboys go.
Where fox and hare make cave and stay,
Dirt and dust are not swept away.
Wasteland in ridges is plowed and tilled,
And plots with vegetables filled.
The emperors of olden days
Are turned now into clods of clays.
Thinking of the sage out of view,
Can I not grieve for old and new?

Su Boyu's Wife

LETTER TO SU BOYU

Atop trees high Sadly birds cry;

In water deep Fatted carps leap.

In empty house Would starve a mouse.

A poor clerk's wife Leads lonely life:

Outdoor I sight A man in white;

But it's not he So dear to me.

I come indoor And I deplore,

West I step forth To the hall north.

I ply my loom To dispel gloom.

Deeply I sigh. Who will reply?

Since our adieu I long for you.

You went to roam, When to come home?

Like girdle's knot You're not forgot.

You forget me:

Heaven can see.

If I forget you,

Punishment's due.

My conduct's fit,

You should know it.

Like gold it's bright,

Like silver whites.

High as hills steep,

Low as vale deep.
I write to Su
Whose name's Boyu.
He's talent wise,
Which none denies.
His home is in Chang'an,
But himself in Sichuan.
Why should he spare his steed
And not come home with speed?
I've kept for him sheep fine
And many jars of wine.
I've kept millet and wheat
For his fat horse to eat.
Men of today,
—What can I say?—
Can see no light
In what I write.
I begin from the core
And end in corners four.

Liu Kun (271–318)

RIDING THE WIND

At dawn from northern gate we go;
We reach Riverside Hill at night.
In my left hand I bend my bow;
I brandish my sword in my right.
I look back on the palace high;
My cab runs up and down the mountain.
Leaning on saddle, long I sigh;
My tears stream down like flowing fountain.
My steed unsaddled 'neath pine-trees,
I tether it atop the hill.
So sad and drear blows autumn breeze;
In cold clear stream flows water chill.
Waving my hand, so sad I feel;
Sobbing, to speak I am not free.
The floating clouds seem to congeal;
The homing birds wheel round for me.
Farther away from home each day,
How long can I still play my part?
Inflamed in the wood on my way,
I stroke my knees with broken heart.
Before me to and fro deer run;
Monkeys and apes play by my side.

Since food resources have been done,
Could we live on ferns far and wide?
I order soldiers, reins in hand;
Among the crags I croon and roar.
His way not followed in this land,
What could be done by Master[1] poor?
I still remember General Li[2]
Captured by Huns with main and might,
And punished for his loyalty;
The emperor had no clear sight.
I try to finish this refrain,
So sad that I put it apart;
So long I wont't sing it again,
For fear lest it should break my heart.

---

[1] Confucius.

[2] General Li Ling fought against hopeless odds and was defeated by the Huns and punished by Emperor Wu of Han (156-87 BC).

Guo Pu (276–324)

SONG OF IMMORTALS

The gallants live in capital;

The hermits' huts in forest stand.

Why should you envy lordly hall

Not lasting as the fairy land?

Drink water clear by riverside;

Pluck herbs divine on mountains proud!

Dragons in water deep may hide.

Why should you climb up floating cloud?

Zhuang Zhou[1] declined an office high;

Lai's wife retired to mountains deep.[2]

The dragon might go up the sky;

You'd sink and be caught like a sheep.

Better soar o'er the world in breeze

And o'erdo the hermits with ease!

---

[1] Zhuang Zhou was a philosopher.

[2] Old Lai was a hermit.

Wang Xizhi[1] (321–379)

IN ORCHID PAVILION

All scenes are vivified in spring;
We share our joy with everything.
Above, we see the azure sky;
Below, the stream's green waves flow by.
The vast expanse is fine and bright;
What meets our eyes shows us the light.
Nature is great and fair and square;
Different things have equal share.
Though high and low they grow in view,
For me there is nothing but new.

---

[1] Wang Xizhi was a famous calligrapher, drinking wine and making verse together with forty poets, including Xie An, in Orchid Pavilion on the third day of the third lunar month in 353.

Xie An, Xie Lang, Xie Daoyun[1]

SNOW

To what may be compared a skyful of white snow?

(Xie An)

It is like handfuls of salt in the air we throw.

(Xie Lang)

Or wind-borne willow catkins wafting high and low.

(Xie Daoyun)

---

[1] Xie An was prime minister and Xie Xuan was his nephew, cornmander-in-chief of the Southern army which fought against heavy odds and beat the Northern army in 383. Xie Lang was also his nephew and Xie Daoyun his niece.

Gu Kaizhi[1] (345–406)

SPIRIT OF THE FOUR SEASONS

Spring water overbrims the streams;
Summer cloud fancy peaks outshines;
The autumn moon sheds brilliant beams;
On winter cliffs stand cold-proof pines.

---

[1] Gu Kaizhi was a famous painter of the Jin dynasty and these four verses were written respectively on four of his pictures.

Tao Qian (365–427)

Spring Excursion

I

Seasons pass by,
Smiles this fine day.
In spring dress, I
Go eastward way.
Peaks steeped in cloud,
In mist veiled spring.
South wind flaps loud
O'er sprouts like wing.

II

In wide lake green
I steep my knee.
On happy scene
I gaze with glee.
As people say,
Content brings ease.
With wine I stay
Drunk as I please.

III

I gaze mid-stream
And miss the sages
Singing their dream
Of Golden Ages.
How I adore
Their quiet day!
Their time's no more
And gone for aye.

IV

In light or gloom,
I rest at ease
'Mid grass and bloom,
Bamboos and trees,
A lute on bed,
A jar of wine.
Golden Age's fled,
Alone I pine.

A Trip to the Slanting Stream

Five days of the new year have passed;
My life is drawing near the last.
Can I not free my heart from sorrow?
We make this trip before tomorrow.
Steeped in fresh air and bright sunbeam,
We sit along the rippling stream.
In sparkling waves breams swim with pleasure;
In quiet vales gulls scream at leisure.
The brimming lake arrests the eye;
I muse on the pagoda high.
Though not so high as the Ninth Tier,
It commands a view without peer.
I pass the jar of wine around,
And ask friends in wine to be drowned.
I know not if another day
We can enjoy still in this way.
Half drunk, we may blow hot or cold,
Forgetting the sorrow age-old,
If we can enjoy our fill but now,
Oh, let tomorrow knit its brow!

A SOUTHERN COMPLAINT

The way to Heaven's dim and far.

Who knows what gods and spirits are.

At fifteen I learned to do good,

At fifty-four I passed manhood.

While young, I went a rugged way;

Mu lute-string broke before its day.

The burning sun scorched my fields;

The insects damaged my corn yields.

The wind and rain raged up and down;

I could not reap half I have sown.

Hunger stared me at summer's height;

Cold bed frozen me in winter night.

At dusk I waited for cocks to crow,

At dawn for the sun to sink low.

Not Heaven but I am to blame;

What e'er I do, I'm still the same.

What matters the fame after death?

It will vanish like smoke or breath.

Alone I pour out plaintive song.

Will connoisseurs listen for long?

Reply to Pang

Friends may not be acquaintances old;
Chance meeting may warm winter cold.
If we enjoy the same delight,
Your visit beautifies the site.
We talk unlike the vulgar kind,
The sage will elevate our mind.
When we have a jar of good wine,
Home brew would become drink divine.
A lonely hermit fond of rest,
I go no longer east or west.
All men love new things and friends old.
Let news in black and white be told.
Though severed by mountains and streams,
We're joined in the heart shedding beams
You love a rural life, but when,
In which year can we meet again?

WRITTEN ON THE 1ST DAY OF THE 5TH MOON IN THE SAME RHYMES AS SECRETARY DAI

Time flies like an empty boat with swift oar;

Four seasons circulate and reappear.

Looking back, the New Year's Day is no more;

Now we come near the middle of the year.

By southern window there're no withered trees;

In northern grove we find leaves lush and green.

Morning seems beautified by summer breeze,

And timely rain washes the country clean.

Who comes on earth shall go, such is our fate,

And what begins will end, such is our life.

Though changeless, for the changeful we may wait;

Content with poverty won't lead to strife.

Our life is full of weal and woe,

On ups and downs our mind can't rest.

If we don't care for what is high or low,

Why should we climb to mountain crest?

IN REPLY TO LIU OF CHAISANG

Hills and lakes attract me for long.

Should I stay away from their song?

It's for my kinsmen near and dear

That nowhere else I would appear.

Fine morning enters curious breast,

Cane in hand, I head for Cot West.

Along the way no passers-by

But ruined huts arrest the eye.

I have repaired my thatched cot,

And ploughed new furrows in my plot.

When valley wind turns chill at first,

I drink spring wine to quench my thirst.

A daughter cannot help as man,

But she will comfort as she can.

The court affairs seem far away

From us with each year and each day.

I plough and weave enough for me;

From other needs I am carefree.

A hundred years will come to end,

Then life and fame with death will blend.

REPLY TO LIU, PREFECT OF CHAISANG

Living unsociable behind closed gate,
I care not how four seasons circulate.
When I see fallen leaves along the way,
I sigh for the coming of autumn day.
Gloomy marrows at northern wall vibrate,
And paddy fields in the south undulate.
If I do not enjoy delight, then how
Can I know next year as happy as now?
So I tell wife and children to go out
To climb a hill or wander thereabout.

In Reply to Secretary Guo

I. Summer

The shady trees before my hall
Store coolness against summer heat.
The south wind comes at season's call,
My lapel welcomes its breath sweet.
Not sociable even at leisure,
I rise to play my lute or read.
Eating my garden greens with pleasure,
I've stored up a year's grain and seed.
I won't lead a life beyond measure.
Why should I have more than I need?
I pound sorghum to make home brew;
And drink until in wine I'm drowned.
Beside me plays my son of two,
Making inarticulate sound.
Such trifling things afford delight;
I forget the vainglorious age.
Gazing from afar on clouds white,
I seem to see the ancient sage.

II. AUTUMN

Three spring moons abound in mild rain;

Now come the cool, pure autumn days.

No mist floats over dewy plain;

The sky sublime sheds limpid rays.

Peaks tower, mountains undulate,

What a wonderful far-off sight!

Chrysanthemums are golden mate

Of green pines crowning rocky height.

On their spirit I meditate:

Frost-proof, they are so brave and bright.

Cup in hand, I miss the recluse

Who loved blooms and pines long ago.

What have I done? What could I choose?

I can only bend my head low.

FOR MY COUSIN JINGYUAN

I've hidden in thatched cot secluded trace;
From social life I stay far, far away.
Left and right I find no familiar face;
My wicket gate is closed e'en at midday.
The dreary wind mourns the end of the year;
From dawn till dusk falls a skyful of snow.
I listen but no sound reaches my ear;
I gaze but see dazzling light high and low.
Chilly air invades my collar and sleeves;
My table's often bare of drink and food.
In empty rooms only solitiude grieves.
What's there to please? Can there be nothing good?
I can peruse but books of olden days,
In which I find deeds worthy of memory.
I cannot climb the old time-honored ways,
Though wrongly praised for honest poverty.
If I can't follow the broad common road,
Is it bad a rural life to renew?
I tell you I will not leave my abode,
Who can understand me better than you?

ON MY RIVER JOURNEY

While young, I used to be carefree,
Only indulged in lute and books.
Plain dress did not reduce my glee,
Nor did course food impair my looks.
As chance would have it, disinclined
I drove up my official way.
Staff in hand, I made up my mind
To leave my garden for a day.
Far, far away goes my lonely boat;
Long, long my home thoughts haunt my heart.
Is it not a long journey afloat?
A thousand miles keep us apart,
Changing river scenes tire the eye;
Of hillside cot my mind still dreams.
Seeing birds and clouds, I feel shy
And envy fish swimming in streams.
To nature I've ever been true.
Who says my mind is matter-bound?
But the current I must go through,
Then in seclusion I'll be found.

QIAN STREAM REVISITED

How long have I not visited here?
Days have piled up into a year.
Dawn to dusk I see hills and streams,
Scenes are revived as in old dreams.
In fine rain steeped the branches high,
Wind-borne birds ripple cloudy sky.
That's what a familiar eye sees,
Not saddened by a heartfelt breeze.
Why should I plod along the way,
Tied down to my post all the day?
My body seems bound up in view,
But I've a heart none could subdue.
I miss my rural life and song.
Could I be kept away for long?
In homing boat I'd be carefree,
Oh, as a frost-proof cypress tree.

HOME-GOING-AND-COMING SONG

Let me go home!

Oh, why should I still roam,

While my fields will be overgrown with weed?

Why don't I go where there is need?

Since I allowed my body to be master of my mind,

Why should my service be considered as unkind?

Let the bygone days be bygone!

The future's still my own.

I've not gone far astray,

Now that I know I was wrong yesterday.

My boat and ripples sway;

My robe flaps with breeze light.

I ask my homeward way,

And wait to see twilight.

Seeing my cot with glee,

I'm afraid to be late.

My household welcomes me

With children at the gate.

The paths look like wasteland

But for chrysanthemum and pine.

I enter, holding my youngest son's hand,
And see my cup brimming with wine.
I freely drink unoccupied,
And gaze with smile at courtyard trees.
Standing by the window with pride,
In narrow rooms I feel at ease.
I walk in my garden with pleasure;
The gate is closed without a bar.
Wandering, staff in hand, at leisure,
I look upward and afar.
Carefree clouds leave the mountain crest,
Tired birds fly back towards their nest.
The sun is dimmed on its decline,
And I caress a lonely pine.
I'm now at home,
In mundane world I'll no more roam.
Since social life and I cannot agree,
What can I seek to do if I want to be free?
Talking with kins will bring me pleasure;
Reading and playing lute beguile my leisure.
I'm told by farmers of the coming of season best
For me to till the field in the west.

I drive a cart

Or row a boat.

To go across rugged hills I start,

Or on a winding stream I float.

With joy all flowers blow;

Slowly streams glide from fountains clear.

In time all the things move and grow;

To the end my life's drawing near.

So let it be!

How long on earth can I do what I please?

Why not set my mind free?

Where should I go? Why ill at ease?

I do not aspire to wealth or renown,

Nor go up to celestial spheres.

I only wish to wander on my own

Or leave my staff to till the field where weed appears.

I'll go up eastern hill to sing

Or croon a verse by limpid stream.

I'll return to the source of spring

And vanish with sunshine or moonbeam.

Body, Shadow and Spirit
I. Body to Shadow

The sky and earth will last forever;
Streams flow and mountains spread as ever.
As a rule, drooping plants may renew,
Withered by frost and revived by dew.
If man is the wisest of all,
Can he not know who rise will fall?
A man whom we have seen before
May die at once and is no more.
But who will take note of his death for long?
Even his kins have no memory strong.
Only the things he left before their eyes
May draw from them sad tears and drear sighs.
To be immortal I don't know the art,
Nor do I doubt of my alloted part.
I wish you would remember what I say;
And drink our cup of wine without delay.

II. SHADOW TO BODY

A man's life cannot last forever;

It is hard even to live long.

You like immortal land as ever.

Can you tell the way not to go wrong?

Our companionship may not fade,

For we have shared same joy and pain.

If I have left you in the shade,

In sunshine I'll appear again.

We can't get together forever;

In time we both shall disappear.

Could I stay when you are gone? Never.

Thinking of this, I'm sad and drear.

But good deeds will be left tomorrow.

Why then do you not do your best?

Though drinking may drive away sorrow,

What good has wine done to your rest?

III. Spirit

Impartial is Heaven's power high,
All things follow its laws divine.
Man levels up with earth and sky.
Is it not due to power mine?
Different beings as we are,
Still we're Three united in One.
We live and die under same star,
And know how to end what's begun.
The three great emperors were sages,
But where can they be found today?
The oldest Peng had lived eight ages,
And could not have a longer stay.
Young and old will die in the end;
Wit and fool may have the same fate.
Wine may make you forget, not mend.
Won't it make death precipitate?
Doing good will gladden your mind.
Who'll sing after your death your praise?
Do not think of things of such kind,
But follow nature in future days.
Play with rising or ebbing tide
Without pleasure and without fear!
Enjoy sunny as shady side!
Let things appear and disappear!

WRITTEN AT LEISURE ON DOUBLE NINTH DAY

Life is short, full of cares and sighs;
On earth men still wish to live long.
In time sun and moon sink and rise,
But we like the Double Ninth song.
The wind won't sough on dreary dew;
The fresh air makes the sky more clear.
Parting swallows leave no shadow new;
Honking wild geese don't reach the ear.
Drinking may drive all cares away;
Chrysanthemums prolong our life.
Living in thatched cot night and day.
I still neglect the world in strife.
Cups would feel ashamed without wine;
Unenjoyed flowers bloom in vain.
Donning my robe, I croon verse line;
Deep thoughts may lead to joy or pain.
Enjoying solitude with pleasure,
I'm happy in my life of leisure.

Return to Nature

I

While young, I was not used to worldly cares,
And hills became my natural compeers.
But by mistake I fell in mundane snares,
And was thus entangled for thirteen years.
A caged bird would long for wonted wood,
And fish in ponds for native pools would yearn.
Go back to till my southern field I would,
To live a rural life why not return?
My plot of ground is but ten acres square;
My thatched cottage has eight or nine rooms.
In front I have peach trees here and plums there;
Over back eaves willows and elms cast glooms.
A village can be seen in distant dark,
Where plumes of smoke rise and waft in the breeze.
In alley deep a dog is heard to bark,
And cocks crow as if over mulberry trees.
Into my courtyard no one should intrude,
Nor rob my private rooms of peace and leisure.
After long, long official servitude,
Again in nature I find homely pleasure.

II

In countryside few care about the State,
Nor wheels nor hooves are heard in the deep gloom
By broad daylight I close my wicket gate;
No worldly dust invades my vacant room.
Sometimes I go along the winding way
And meet with peasants through the bushy field.
Then we have nothing untoward to say
But talk about our corn's growth and its yield.
Our corn grows day by day under our feet;
My field becomes wider beyond wild grass.
But I fear the onset of frost and sleet
Would do harm to my com and grain, alas!

III

I sow my beans 'neath Southern Hill,
Bean shoots are lost where weeds o'er grow.
I weed at dawn though early still;
I plod home with my moonlit hoe.
The path is narrow, grasses tall,
With evening dew my clothes wet,
To which I pay no heed at all,
If my desire can but be met.

IV

Having long left hills and streams, how
I love to roam in woody place!
Coming with sons and nephews, now
Through hazels I see ruined trace.
I pace up and down on waste land
And find debris of dwellers old.
Marks of old wells and stoves still stand,
Dead branches are left in the cold.
I ask a woodman passing by,
If he knows who lived here before.
The woodman answers with a sigh,
"They are all dead and gone, no more."
Thirty years passed in town and court,
Everything has changed, it is true.
Life is a vison fair and short;
All will vanish into the blue.

V

Melancholy, I come back, staff in hand,

Going alone the rugged bushy way.

In mountain crooks shallow and clear I stand

And wash my feet where a moment I stay.

At home I strain my newly-ripened wine,

Cook a chicken and with neighbors share it.

My room turns dark when there's no more sunshine,

Branches are burned instead of candle lit.

So joyful we're that we find short the night;

Soon in the east we see the first sunlight.

BEGGING FOR FOOD

Driven by hunger, I go out
But I do not know whereabout.
I plod on and on till this land;
I knock and speechless there I stand.
The host, seeing my hidden pain,
Gives me food lest I'd come in vain.
We talk until the sun's decline;
We empty cup on cup of wine.
I'm glad to make acquaintance new;
I write this verse as it is due.
I can't repay like Han Xin[1] fed
By a washerwoman her bread.
How to express my hearty thanks?
In underworld on griefless banks[2].

---

[1] While young, Han Xin (2nd century B.C.) was fed by a washerwoman.
When he became a general, he repaid her kindness with gold.
[2] It was believed in ancient China that there was a Griefless River in the
underworld.

DRINKING ALONE ON RAINY NIGHTS

Where there's life, there will be death:
This truth is well known since old days.
Where can we find immortal breath
Exhaled in superhuman ways?
Old friends tell me a jar of wine
Would make me forget weal and woe.
After drinking nectar divine,
Even to Heaven I won't go.
Is Heaven far from our good earth?
Following nature, you'll go high.
The crane in cloud with wings of worth
Flies to and fro from earth to sky.
I have been firm in my belief
And in my life for forty years.
My mind is free of joy and grief,
Though long my body changed appears.

MOVING HOUSE

In Southern Village I would dwell,
Not that the house there augurs well,
But people live in simple ways,
With whom I'm glad to pass my days.
For years I've cherished this ideal;
Today it becomes true and real.
Why should I need a spacious flat
But room enough for bed and mat?
My neighbors may call now or then,
And talk of olden days and men.
We'll read good writings we enjoy
And solve the questions which annoy.

MY COTTAGE CAUGHT FIRE IN MID-SUMMER (AD. 408)

Living in thatched cot down shabby lane,

I loved it more than house of golden frames

A mid-summer blast blew with might and main,

My hut in the glade was swept by the flames

My rooms were all burned up and lost to sight,

So in a boat I sought for shelter soon.

Long, long lasts the new autumn night,

Bright, bright shines the nearly full moon.

Again vegetables begin to grow,

But frightened birds won't come back here.

Far, far away my thoughts at midnight go,

When I gaze on the ninth celestial sphere.

While young, I loved to hold my own,

In that way I've passed forty years.

My body follows up and down,

My mind to independence steers.

It's pure and strong in its own way,

Like jade or stone which is fire-proof.

Looking up, I think of old day

With crops not stored under the roof.

People well-fed were carefree then.
They rose at dawn and slept at night.
Such golden age won't come again,
I would till my land if I might.

DRINKING WINE

I

All men who rise will then decline,
Such is your fate as well as mine.
The melon-grower in the field
Was noble lord who would not yield.
Winter replaces summer days,
Such is the world and all men's ways.
The wise men who find the truth out,
Will not again put it in doubt.
Fill our cup of wine with delight,
Be intoxicated day and night!

IV

A lonely, dreary bird astray
Still flies near the end of the day.
It hovers here and there, its cries
Have darkened night and saddened skies.
Is it longing for morning clear
Or a resting tree far or near?
Seeing a pine of towering height,
Folding its wings, it will alight.
No tree can stand a furious blast,
Which this shady pine can outlast.
The bird has found on it a nest,
For a long time here it will rest.

V

In people's haunt I build my cot,
Of wheel's and hoofs noise I hear not.
How can it leave on me no trace?
Secluded heart makes secluded place.
I pick chrysanthemums at will,
Carefree, I see the Southern Hill.
The mountain air is fresh day and night,
Together birds go home in flight.
What revelation at this view?
Words fail me if I try to tell you.

VII

Lovely chrysanthemums have autumn hue,
I pluck their fresh petals impearled with dew.
Dew-sweetened wine would drive sorrow away.
How could worldly cares in my heart still stay!
Although I drink with no one by my side,
Wine pours out from the pot when cup is dried.
All the bustle sinks with the sinking sun,
Birds flying to the woods sing on the run.
Proudly I croon in eastern corridor,
Glad to find a nearly lost day once more.

VIII

In eastern garden stands a pine-tree green,
Its beauty veiled by shrubs cannot be seen.
When other plants are withered in hoar frost,
We find its lofty branch which seems long lost.
No trees in the woods can attract the eye,
We marvel at the single pine so high.
I stroke its wintry bough, wine pot in hand,
And gaze afar, lost in the wonderland.
Life changes from lost illusion to vain dreams,
Why should I be drowned in eventful streams?

IX

Hearing a knock at dawn while still at rest,

I got up to open, not yet half dressed.

Asking the early comer, "Who are you?"

I saw a smiling farmer come in view.

He came to see me with a pot of wine,

Doubting if worldly offer I'd decline.

"You live in rags under a thatched roof.

But how can your cottage be riches-proof?

Since all the world is drifting with the tide,

Could you alone stand aloft and aside?"

I thank the farmer for his kind advice,

But it's my freedom I won't sacrifice.

Though I may learn to go official way,

To do against my will, can I not stray?

Let us rejoice at drinking the cup dry!

I won't go backward as the days go by.

X

In bygone days I traveled far and wide,
Nearly as far as the eastern seaside.
Can I forget my journey hard and long,
Impeded by heavy rain and wind strong?
For what should I have gone such a long way,
Were I not driven by hunger I'd stay?
I did my best to get my daily meal,
A little bit seemed to me a great deal.
Afraid no office work was worth my strife,
I would go back to live my rural life.

XIII

Two men who live under one and same roof
Go different ways apart and aloof.
A man of letters drunken would appear;
A man of arms stays sober all the year.
They talk and laugh each at the other's way
Of living and seem to laugh it away.
How foolish is a man laden with care!
How proud is the man who drinks in the air!
I would like to tell the drinker to light
A candle so as to drink in the night.

XIV

Old friends who know my love of wine
Come, bottle in hand, to see me.
We sit on bushes beneath the pine,
After a few rounds drunk are we.
All at once old men chat away;
Out of tune we pass round the cup.
We know not who we are today.
Can we value what's down or up?
Long, long we are lost in the drink;
In the delight of wine we sink.

XVI

While young, I had social relation cold,
And only indulged in six classics old,
Now I am nearly forty years of age,
But life does not turn for me a new page.
I did not fear all my life to be poor.
Could I suffer from hunger any more?
My wretched cottage hears grievous wind pass,
My front yard buried in weeds and grass.
I don my coat to stay the long, long night;
My cock won't crow to welcome morning light.
If ancient connoisseur Meng were near me,
To tell him what I feel I would be free.

XVII

Sweet orchid in the front yard grows,
With fragrance waiting for the breeze.
The welcome breeze rises and blows,
Sweeping the weeds breeding disease.
In life's journey I lost my way
Until I see a gleam of light.
I know I'd hide my bow and stay
At home when there's no bird in flight.

XIX

Underfed for long in my native land,
I left the hoe to take the pen in hand.
I had not enough to feed my household.
Could we not suffer from hunger and cold?
When I was nearly thirsty years of age,
I felt ashamed to face the ancient sage.
Then I resolved to go my former way,
To live a rural life to end my day.
Star on star breathes an air current high;
Year by year a dozen springs have gone by.
The way of the world is so wide and long,
Even a philosopher would go wrong.
Though I have no gold to provide a feast,
I may drink cups of home-made wine at least.

XX

Far, far away ancient emperors' days,

No one still lives in their natural ways.

Confucius taught disciples without rest

To purify the world from east to west.

Though the auspicious bird did not alight,

They tried still to renew music and rite.

But two River songs were not heard to sing,

The stream of time passed till the tyrant king,

Who ordered *Books of Poetry* should be burned,

And no more classics should again be learned.

Only a few old scholars tried to spread

The six Confucian classics to be read.

Why then after the Han dynasty's fall

Would no scholar study Six Books at all?

So many chariots run all the day long,

But nowhere is heard the sagacious song.

If I did not drink my fill, free from care,

Could I be worthy of the hood I wear?

But I regret the mistakes I have made.

Would you forgive what a drunkard has said?

ABSTINENCE

Living within the city bound,
I pass my days freely at leisure.
I take a seat on shady ground,
Or stroll within the gate with pleasure.
I only eat my herbage fine
And enjoy playing with my son.
I never abstain from drinking wine:
Without wine, life is joyless one,
At night in bed I can't well stay,
Nor can I rise with rising sun.
If I abstain from day to day,
No harm to my health will be done.
I knew that unhappy I'd feel,
But not what good is done to me.
Now I know abstinence brings weal,
I will abstain today with glee.
If I could abstain as I'm told
Until I reach celestial spheres,
A young look would replace the old
And youth might last a thousand years.

BLAMING SONS

My temples covered with white hair,
My skin wrinkled, my muscles slack.
Though I have five sons, none would care
To read or write in white or black.
My eldest son is now twice eight,
But lazy as him none appears.
My second son won't dedicate
Himself to arts at fifteen years.
My third and fourth sons at thirteen
Know not how much makes six plus seven.
My youngest son has nine years green;
'Mid pears and nuts he is in heaven.
If such be the decree divine,
What can I do but drink my wine?

OLD-STYLED VERSE

IV

The hundred-foot-high tower proud
Commands superb views far and nigh.
At dusk it's crowned with drowsy cloud,
At dawn around it birds will fly.
Mountain on mountain, stream on stream,
All come in sight with boundless plain.
Heroes of yore with smile would beam
To win victory and glory vain.
They would die in a hundred years
And lie buried then underground.
Cypress or pine felled disappears,
Lofty tomb leveled down to mound.
A fallen empire has no heir,
Where could the roaming soul be found?
Glory is a castle in the air;
There is no hero but death-bound!

MISCELLANEOUS POEMS

I

A man is rootless in his day,
Floating like dust along the way.
Blown east and west, no longer am I
Still the same as in days gone by.
When born, I may be called your brother,
Why then should we not love each other?
Let us enjoy when days are fine,
Call neighbors out to drink our wine!
The prime of our life won't come twice;
Each day can't have two mornings nice.
I urge you to rise with the sun,
For time and tide will wait for none.

II

Beyond the western hills sinks the sun white;
Over east ridge the moon sheds her pure light.
For miles and miles overflow the moonbeams;
The air is permeated with shadows and dreams.
With the west wind my lonely room is filled;
At dead of night my mat and pillow chilled.
In autumn's breath I hear seasonal song;
On sleepless bed I feel the night so long.
I want to talk, but to whom to confide?
I drink to lonely shadow by my side.
The sun and the moon rise and fall with speed,
But where can I gallop at will my steed?
Thinking of this, I am so much depressed.
How could my mind all the night long find rest!

III

Prosperity cannot last long;

Rise and fall alternate their song.

Lotus flowers bloom after spring,

But autumn will lotus seed bring.

When grass is bitten by hoar frost,

The lotus withers, though not lost.

Sun and moon set and again rise;

None can revive after he dies.

From olden memories awoken,

Oh, how could my mind not be broken!

IV

A lofty man should benefit four seas,

But I'd enjoy till old a life of ease.

I'd have my kinsmen under the same roof,

And all my children safe and sound, harm-proof.

I croon and play my lute morning or night;

My wine cup never dried affords delight.

Freely I'd drink my fill with loose belt ties;

Early I'd go to bed and late to rise.

Can I be like those who would climb up higher,

Worried for gain and loss like ice and fire?

All will be buried in the grave in time.

Why should we care for glory, though sublime!

V

I still remember in my prime
I could be happy in sad time.
Over the four seas I aimed high;
Spreading my wing I dreamed to fly.
But youthful days passed and grew old,
My zeal for life as soon turned cold.
Delightful things were not enjoyed;
Worries and cares often annoyed.
I feel my youthful strength no more,
Each day not as the day before.
Time like a stream will pass away,
And leads me on without delay.
How far ahead should I still float?
I know not where to moor my boat.
The ancients had no time to waste.
How can late-comers make no haste?

VI

When elders talked of bygone years,

Displeased, I would shut up my ears.

But fifty years have gone by now,

And time writes wrinkles on my brow.

I would recall youthful delight,

But I can find no pleasure slight.

Far, far away are bygone days.

Could I relive in olden ways?

To drink my fill I'd spare no gold;

I would keep pace with days grown old.

I'd leave no money for my sons;

There's no need if they're worthy ones.

VII

The sun and moon will not slow down;
Four seasons press each other on.
The chilly wind strips trees away,
Fallen leaves strewn along the way.
My health turns weak with worsened fate;
My black hair has whitened of late.
Of age my head bears the pale sign,
My forward way on the decline.
My home becomes an inn for rest;
The dweller's rather like a guest.
Oh, where, oh, where can I go still?
To the graveyard 'neath southern hill.

VIII

I do not hope to earn good wages;
To do farm work is all my due.
My folks have tilled the field for ages;
Hunger and cold are nothing new.
I never ask more than enough,
Satisfied with chaff and plain food,
Clad in winter clothes of poor stuff
And in summer garment not so good.
I cannot meet my humble need.
How sad to say with broken heart!
Others may thrive in word or deed,
I can't earn a living apart.
What can I do and how can I
Drown my grief but drink my cup dry!

A Poor Scholar

Every thing has its resting place;
Alone the cloud's drifting in vain.
Melting in air, it leaves no trace.
When can we see its glow again?
Morning clouds rise from mist of night,
All birds fly to welcome the day.
One in the woods is late in flight,
But early on its homeward way.
I'll keep to beaten track of yore,
Though from hunger and thirst not free,
There're no connoisseurs any more.
Why should poverty sadden me?

READING THE *BOOK OF MOUNTAINS AND SEAS*

In early summer plants and grass grow high;

Around my cottage trees cast leafy shade.

Here birds rejoice to sing their lullaby,

So I love my thatched hut in the glade.

After I've tilled the land and sown the seed,

I may come back to read my books at leisure.

My lane's too humble for carriage and steed,

Where visitors can't find any more pleasure.

Still I am happy to drink my spring wine,

And pluck from my garden the herbage green.

A fine rain from the east tries to combine

With a fair breeze to beautify the scene.

I read the myth of legendary king

And the Book with Maps of Mountains and Seas.

I see the ups and downs from spring to spring.

What is happier than to do what I please?

An Elegy for Myself

Where there is life, there must be death;
In due time we'll breathe our last breath.
Last night we lived and filled our posts;
Today my name's among the ghosts,
Where is my soul fled far away?
But shriveled forms in coffin stay.
My children miss their father, crying;
My friends caress my body, sighing.
For gain or loss I no more care;
Right or wrong is not my affair.
Thousands of years will pass away,
And shame and glory of today.
But I regret, while living still,
I have not drunk wine to my fill.

Xie Lingyun[1] (385–433)

PASSING MY ANCESTRAL ESTATE

While young, I would be right and fair,

But tarried then in worldly care against my will till yesterday,

When twenty years have passed away.

Blackened and ground, can I be bright?

Tired and spent, I'm shamed by the upright.

Now dull and ill, I come again to see my quiet old domain.

Ordered to rule over the seaside,

To my ancestral house I ride. I come uphill and down the vale;

Upstream and downstream I set sail.

High mountains spread for miles and miles;

The stream is dotted with isles on isles.

White clouds embrace the boulders steep;

Green ripples lull bamboos to sleep.

I will rethatch my roof and rest

In my cottage on mountain crest.

To villagers I wave my hand:

"In three years I'll come to this land.

Try to plant elms and coffin-trees!

Don't neglect this wish of mine, please!"

---

[1] Xie Lingyun was grandson of Xie Xuan, commander-in-chief of the
Southern army which fought against heavy odds and defeated the Northern
army in 383. Not duly employed in the Song dynasty, he became governor
over the seaside in 422, where Xie An and Xie Xuan had built their family
estate. Discontented, he was punished with death in 433.

Out of West Archery Hall at Dusk

Out of the town gate in the west,
I gaze afar where mountains loom.
I see cliff on cliff, crest on crest,
The deep blue sinks into the gloom.
Maple leaves reddened by hoar frost,
Evening crags exhale misty breath.
In seasons past my grief is lost;
I seem to feel my sorrow's depth.
A lonely hen yearns for her mate,
A bird astray longs for a nest.
Even they've feelings delicate.
Can I not think of my dear best?
My mirrored hair sprinkled with grey,
The belt around my waist turns loose.
To follow nature is my way;
To play my lute is what I choose.

ON POOLSIDE TOWER

The coiling dragon hides with ease;

The honking swan's heard far and wide.

I can't float like cloud as I please,

Nor sink nor swim by riverside.

I can't advance for lack of wit,

To retire to plow I'm not good,

To return to seaside I'm fit;

I lie sick, facing empty wood.

Ignoring seasons on my pillows,

I open door despite my ills.

I give ear to the surging billows,

And feast my eyes on craggy hills.

In early spring no cold winds blow;

The new sun dispels shadows old.

By poolside vernal grasses grow;

On willows sing birds manifold,

I'm moved by ancient vernal song;

I'd live 'mid green grass as I please.

Living apart, I can last long;

But hermits cannot take their ease,

Since ancient sages lived well this way,

Why should it grieve those of today?

A Lonely Islet in the River

Tired of familiar Southern view,
I have neglected the Northern shore.
Long is the way to seek what's new,
I find unusual scenes no more.
Suddenly when the waves are crossed,
The stream's charmed by a lonely isle.
The azure sky in water lost,
The sun and white clouds beam with smile.
When beauty's not enjoyed in time,
What of hidden truth can we say?
I think of Mount Kunlun sublime,
From human world so far away.
I believe the immortal's art
Will purify a troubled heart.

MOUNT STONE DRUM

Depressed on life's journey for long,

I feel sorrow on sorrow strong.

My native land so far away;

Streams and hills my journey delay.

Ill at ease, how to spend my leisure?

In early spring I climb for pleasure.

My homesickness can't be consoled,

I'll climb to drown my sorrow old.

How vast the eastern country looks;

I turn and find a narrow west.

The setting sun ripples the brooks,

And cloud on cloud forms crest on crest.

White clovers vie in their shoots new,

And green duckweeds push leaf on leaf.

Flowers can't please me with their hue,

Seeking delight, I'm drowned in grief.

I gaze afar, but all in vain.

What is the use to gaze again?

Written on the Lake, Returning from Stone Cliff

The weather changes morning and night;
Mountain and lake with radiance beam.
Their radiance clear gives me delight;
I forget to go home downstream.
I left the vale the sun still crowned;
At sunset I come back by boat.
In twilight woods and vale are drowned;
In evening mist colored clouds float.
Green lotus leaves and caltrops sway;
Dark reeds and cattails lean before.
I hurry back on southern way;
Happy, I rest behind east door.
Unworried, you make light of things;
Content, you won't go against reason.
If you want to live long, long springs,
Please try to take my word in season!

JOURNEY ACROSS THE MOUNTAIN AND ALONG THE BROOK

The dawn announced by gibbons' cry,
No light's dispelled the valley's gloom.
Clouds gathered now beneath cliffs high,
Dew glistens on flowers in bloom.
I go the way through nook and crook
Towards the far-off mountain crest.
Shoes drenched, I cross the rapid brook
And scale cliff-ladders without rest.
Dotted with sandbars, wind the streams;
I cannot see the forward way.
With floating duckweed the brook teems,
Over clear shallows rushes sway.
I drink on tiptoe flying fountain
And climb a tree to pluck leaves new.
I fancy Goddess of the Mountain
In fig and ivy leaves in view.
I break off hemp, orchids in hand.
To whom to offer? I'm not sure.
Who appreciate will understand.
But who can discern things obscure?
The scenery makes me carefree
And drives sorrow away from me.

Passing the Pavilion on Sandy Shore

Sleeves brushed, I go along the sandy stream;

Slowly I enter the thatched cot alone.

Through scattered trees far-off green mountains gleam;

A nearby creek trickles over stone on stone.

It is hard to describe the void so blue,

But easy to put down a fisherman's song.

The ivy grasped, green cliffs come into view,

My heart blends with spring to which I belong.

Hear orioles wail on jujube tree

And gaily call the grazing deer.

I am now sad now glad to see

Suffering or offering appear.

Weal and woe may now come now go;

Poor or rich, you'll feel grief or joy.

If you are free from weal and woe,

Then you will not be Fortune's toy.

PASSING A NIGHT ON MOUNT STONE GATE

At dawn I gathered orchids proud,
Afraid they'd wither in the frost.
At night I rest amid the cloud,
Enjoying rocks in moonlight lost.
Roosting birds sing their lullaby;
The rising wind hastens leaves' fall.
Different songs come far and nigh;
Melodies are clear one and all.
I can enjoy the night with none,
So I drink alone my sweet wine.
I wait in vain for the Fair One.
Who would dry my hair in sunshine?

Entering Pengli Lake

I'm tired of river journey long;
It's hard to paint the wind and tide.
Split by islets, streams join again;
Waves crash against craggy lakeside.
I hear moonlit gibbons' sad song
And smell sweet iris wet with dew.
Late spring has beautified green plain;
Cliffs tower high, girt with cloud white.
Memories old and images new,
Joy and grief haunt me day and night.
I climb the cliff of Mirror Stone
Through ivy leaves to Gate of Pine.
But find no sages' trace, let slone
The legends of Three Streams or Nine.
The River Gods have secret treasure;
Immortals won't reveal their art.
No golden drug sheds light for pleasure;
No liquid jade flows from warm heart.
In vain I play on lute *the Crane*,
Strings snap and leave parting refrain.

THE YEAR'S END

Deep worried, I can't fall asleep;
I'm pained to see night slowly creep.
The moon shines bright all o'er white snow;
The north wind blows strong out of woe.
World changed, nothing unchanged can stay;
The year passed, life will pass away.

EXCHANGE OF VERSE ON THE STREAM

I. YOUNG MAN

How lovely is the maiden sweet,
Washing in the stream her white feet!
She's like the bright moon o'er the cloud
To reach her I am not allowed.

II. MAIDEN

How pleasing is the young man bright,
Spreading on the stream his sail white!
Should you ask me if you're allowed,
See the moon sinks into the cloud!

Bao Zhao (415–470)

SONG OF NORTHERN FRONTIER

Winged messages came from north frontiers,
Beacon fires seen in capital.
Garrison towns sent cavaliers
To save the north from its downfall.
Late autumn hardened shafts and bows;
The foe's strong in battle array.
Sword in hand, angry the king rose,
Couriers dispatched from day to day.
Men followed the track serpentine;
In single file high bridges they crossed.
Drumbeats and flutes for home would pine;
Armor and flags were clad in frost.
The swift wind swept o'er border plain;
Sand and grit floated high and low.
Stiff as hedgehog spine the horse's mane,
No man could draw the horn-trimmed bow.
In hard times we see men steadfast;
In chaos we know heroes great.
For good rulers lives may be cast
And sacrificed to their dear State.

HARD IS THE WAY
IV

Water spilled on level ground
Will run east, west, north and south bound.
Our life is ruled by fate.
Why should we sigh or grieve early and late?
Let us drink and allay
Our grief and sing no more *Hard Is the Way*!
Though our heart is not stone or wood,
To sing what we feel will do us no good.

THE MUME BLOSSOMS

In midcourt stand manifold trees;
To mume my admiration goes.
Why should you favor it so, please?
Against the cold alone it blows.
It can bear fruit in spite of frost
And dance in wind to greet spring day,
While other blooms in blasts are lost
When from the branches they're torn away.

Farewell to Secretary Fu

In streams and pools the fair swan plays;

On isles and sands the lone goose stays.

Meeting by chance, we know our heart;

We miss each other when apart.

From east to west there're thousand li;

Wind and rain sever you and me.

The bygone time often appears;

Your voices haunt my mind and ears.

The sunset chills isles far and nigh;

The gloomy clouds darken the sky.

My short wings can't fly high and low;

In mist I wander to and fro.

Xie Tiao (464–499)

GRIEF OF A LONELY PALACE MAID

At dusk the palace lowers pearl screen;

No fireflies flicker'mid grass green.

All night she sews her silken gown.

Will royal favor e'er come down?

A LONGING WIFE

With silklike tendrils green grass spread;

On myriad trees bloom flowers red.

Don't tell me you will not come home!

Flowers have fallen when you come.

EXCURSION ON EASTERN FIELDS

Cheerless, I'm dreary beyond measure;
We go hand in hand to seek pleasure.
We enjoy clouds from height to height
And see from hilltop sight on sight.
On gloomy woods I gaze and gaze;
Mist and smoke rise like haze in haze.
Fish play among new lotus leaves;
Birds gone, the fallen flower grieves.
I would not drink sweet vernal wine,
But linger before mountains fine.

RIVER JOURNEY FROM THE WEST TO THE CAPITAL

The Great River flows night and day;

The voyager grieves all the way.

Coming near Purple Mountains strong,

I know the return journey long.

The Milky Way fades in twilight,

Cold riverside still drowned in night.

I crane my neck for capital,

But only see the palace wall.

In golden beams the temple steeps;

O'er royal hall the Jade String[1] peeps.

I drive to the gate of the town,

Missing the tomb of Southern crown.

The sun can't revive ancient graces;

Now east and west, we're in two places.

Wind and cloud can't bar the bird's dream,

But I've no bridge to cross the stream.

I fear attacks of birds of prey;

Chrysanthemums in frost can't stay.

But now the hunters I defy:

I'm flying high in boundless sky.

---

[1] Name of stars.

Gazing at Dusk on the Capital from the Three Peaks

I'm flying high in boundless sky.
Like poets of those bygone days,
Fixing on capital their gaze,
I see afar the high and low.
Winglike tiled roofs in sunset's glow.
The colored clouds spread like brocade;
The river's clear as silver braid.
The islet's loud with birds'spring songs;
The shore's fragrant with blooms in throngs
I linger while going away,
Missing both merry night and day.
When may I come to feast again?
My tears stream down like pearls of rain.
A homesick heart longs to be back.
Could my hair not turn grey from black?

Xiao Yan[1] (464–549)

MIDNIGHT SONGS

I. A SONGSTRESS

Favored, she'd come to me so sweet;

Bashful, she'd make graceful retreat.

She opens rosy lips and sings;

Her jadelike fingers play on strings.

II. A BEAUTY

The morning sun shines on windows green;

The breeze ripples embroidered screen,

Her pearllike teeth smile sweet and tender;

Her eyes bewitch with eyebrows slender.

---

[1] Emperor Wu of the Liang Dynasty.

SONG OF THE SOUTHERN SHORE^①

Flowers of gorgeous hues in royal park displayed,

Full blooms and glistening green leaves hang down light shade.

Hand in hand, in short steps dancers reveal spring heart.

Dancers reveal spring heart

On balmy, palmy days.

Palace maids stand apart

And turn off envious gaze.

---

① This song was said to be the earliest lyric existant.

Fan Yun (451–503)

MOORED AT NEW TOWER

Far trees by riverside

Seem to float on the tide;

Lonely smoke rises high

At the end of the sky.

The river and sky's end

Like trees and smoke will blend,

Where is the river's home?

How long will my sail roam?

FAREWELL TOWN

East and west of the Farewell Town
People part, going up and down.
When I left, like flowers fell snow;
Now I come, like snow flowers blow.

Jiang Yan (444–505)

AFTER PARTING

You left me and went far, alas!
As far as Gate of Wild Geese Pass.
Sandy clouds spread a thousand li!
O when will you come back to me?
It seems yesterday we bade adieu,
But now the eaves are wet with dew.
I care not for grass in decay,
But for you, cold far, far away.
You stay at the end of the sky,
Leaving your lonely wife to sigh
Could I see your face as I please,
I would be cured as by jade-trees.
As duckweeds miss the pool, and vine
The tree, for you I'll ever pine.

Shen Yue (441–512)

ON THE HEIGHT

Don't climb up on the height!
You'll be grieved at the sight.
Hills stretch without an end;
Into the sky streams blend.
Where is the one I miss?
South of Luoyang he is.
I gaze but see him not.
How can he be forgot?

NIGHT AFTER NIGHT[1]

The Silver River[2] bars the sky
The Dipper rises from low to high.
The stars in vain may swim or sink.
O do they know of whom I think?
The lonely lamp sheds its dim lights
I weave till dawn replaces cold night.
To whom to shed my tears and woe?
In vain I sigh to hear cocks crow.

---

[1] Song of a lonely longing for her husband.
[2] Chinese name for the Milky Way.

WILD GEESE ON THE LAKE

Spring pools are filled with water white,

Migrating geese in homeward flight.

When they peck food, cresses appear,

Their wings cold with frost of last year.

In flocks, they swim and ripple stream;

Single, each chases lonely sunbeam.

Hovering, down they will not go;

Rising pell-mell, they form no row.

Together flapping wings,

They fly until their homeland meets the eye.

LAMENT FOR XIE TIAO[①]

Of all the talents the most bright,

His verse vibrated on the height.

As ringing bells his voice was loud;

His thought climbed the wind to the cloud.

Like pine-trees not afraid of frost,

In this unjust world he was lost.

Although his head was laurel-crowned,

He's buried now in the grave mound.

---

① Xie Tiao died in prison after the rebellion of Xiao Yaoguang in 499.

Six Recollections

I. She Came in Beauty

I think of when she came
Up marble steps like bright, bright flame.
Talking long, long of when we parted,
Of sad, sad yearning, broken-hearted,
We were ne'er tired to gaze our fill;
Our hunger often came to nil.

II. She Sat in Beauty

I think how she was seen
Sitting before the dotted screen,
Now four or five songs she would sing;
Now twice or thrice she'd pluck her string.
Smiling, she was beyond compare;
When vexed, more lovable than e'er.

III. She Ate in Beauty

I think of how she ate:
Her face changed color o'er the plate.
She felt too shy to take her seat,
Too bashful to begin to eat.
As if not hungry, she'd not dine,
Too weak to hold her cup of wine.

IV. SHE SLEPT IN BEAUTY

I think of her in bed:

Sleepy, she lowered not her head.

Till coaxed, she'd not undress her gown,

Nor put on pillow her head down.

Ashamed to be seen by her mate,

In candlelight she'd blush and wit.

Liu Yun (465–511)

A SOUTHERN SONG

I pluck on islet white duckweeds;

The vernal sun warms Southern meads.

A friend comes from Lake Dongting's side;

He met my lord on rivers wide.

Why won't my lord come to his mate?

Again spring flowers blossom late.

He won't tell me joy of new love

Has made my lord forget the far-off.

He Xun (?–518)

Reply to Fan Yun

My cot is shaded with leafy trees;
Lush grass would darken doorsteps quiet.
Bright blooms caressed by gentle breeze,
Sunbeams amid flowers run riot.
Missing you, joyless I remain;
Standing alone, I sigh in vain.
With whom can I talk freely long?
I can enjoy but my verse line.
You may make light of your best song.
How dare I match your verse with mine?

At Parting

My heart is laden with cares vain:
For miles and miles alone I'll go.
On darkened stream it threatens rain;
On whitened waves wind starts to blow.

Wu Jun (469–519)

SONG OF SPRING

O where has spring come from to make
Streams ripple and mume blossoms wake?
The clouds have barred green-fretted gate;
The wind's caressed dew-holding plate.
But my fair one cannot be seen,
Veiled by the gauze curtain and screen.
To talk with her I find no way;
In face of lovesick cup I stay.

Wang Ji

ON RIVER YOYA

My leaflike boat floats far and nigh;
The river blends into the sky.
Dim clouds rise from the distant crag;
Bright sunrays chase the stream zigzag.
Mountains and woods seem calmer still
With birds' song and cicadas' trill.
How can I not think of my home?
So many years have I to roam!

Yin Keng (?–565)

CROSSING GREEN GRASS LAKE

On Green Grass Lake spring waves o'er flow;
With outspread sails my boat will go.
The stream in peach blossoms is dyed;
Queen's flowers sweeten riverside.
East, the Immortal Cave is nigh,
West, Peak of Goddess towers high.
The sky purifies water green;
The sun reflected stirs floating sheen.
Sails hang atop the far-off tree;
On dizzy mast alight birds free.
Before the flood I'm at a loss.
Could my leaflike boat go across?

LEAVING NEW TOWER AT DUSK

The great river rolls on with ease;
My parting grief surges without rest.
The tide flows out like canopies;
Clouds rise too dim to form hill-crest.
Drumbeats are heard from far away;
Pine trees are seen on mountains cold.
My journey only done halfway,
Missing New Tower, I grow old.

Chen Shubao[1] (553–604)

BLOOMING JADE TREES IN THE BACKYARD

Blooming trees stand before the splendid palace hall;

There's none but beauties in their new dress would enthral.

With charm congealed, at first they linger at the door;

Bashful out of boudoir, they smile and come before.

Their faces look as pretty as dew-impearled flowers;

Their bodies like jade trees shed light on inner bowers.

---

[1] The last emperor of the Chen dynasty, who was hearing this song written by himself when the Sui army entered his capital and he was made a captive. Hence this song was the symbol of a conquered kingdom.

Xu Ling (507–583)

THE MOON OVER THE MOUNTAIN PASS

The full moon o'er the mountain pass,

A soldier is homesick, alas!

"My longing wife in tower high,

Sleepless at her window, should sigh.

Star-flags unfurled on border west,

Clouds in array sweep mountain crest.

The warts run on from year to year.

When can I not be stationed here?"

Wei Ding^① (515–593)

ON HEARING A BLACKBIRD IN THE NORTH

Scenes change in countries far apart,
At the song of a bird I start.
How can it sing to me who roam,
The song I used to hear at home.

---

① Wei Ding was an envoy of the Southern Kingdom of Chen sent to the
capital of the Northern Zhou.

Wang Bao^① (513–576)

CROSSING THE YELLOW RIVER TO THE NORTH

The autumn breeze blows down sear leaves
As waves of Southern Lake it grieves.
High mountains o'erlook northern land;
On Yellow River remparts stand.
On hearing music strange, I start;
The Sobbing Stream's Song breaks my heart.
At dusk my horse has gone astray;
In Northern Col I've lost my way.

---

① Southern poet who became captive of the Northern emperor.

SEEING A FRIEND OFF SOUTH

A hundred years have left an old tree,

A thousand miles darkens yellow sand.

Nearer the native hills you see;

Watching you farther off, I stand.

Yu Xin (512–580)

REFLECTIONS①

Desolate outposts stretch afar;

The dreary wind blows up sandbar.

The foe runs riot out the walls;

Their shade in Yellow River falls.

The chilly stream has seen friends part

And heroes leave with broken heart.

What could you do with might and main

But sing your farewell song in vain!

The sailor leaves his home at night;

---

① It was written in imitation of Ruan Ji's *Reflections*.

The Moon Viewed from the Boat

He views from his boat the moon bright.

The mountains seem covered with snow;

The sandy shores glitter and glow.

A brilliant pearl is born on high;

With flowers stars sprinkle the sky.

The halo fades around the moon;

Full, it begins to wane alone.

Parting again with Secretary Zhou

On long, long way of Sunny Pass

Alone I can't go back, alas!

Only the riverside wild geese

Fly southward when blows autumn breeze.

Yang Guang[1] (569–618)

THE RIVER ON A MOONLIT NIGHT IN BLOOMING SPRING

The river's calm when ends the day;

Spring flowers bloom by riverside.

The waves carry the moon away;

The stars rise and fall with the tide.

---

① The last emperor of the Sui Dynasty, notorious for his luxurious life.

A FIELD VIEW

Here and there fly a thousand dots of crows;

Around a lonely village water flows,

The slanting sun bids to the day adieu.

How can my heart not break at this sad view!

MIDNIGHT SONG[1]

I cannot sleep in long, long night.
Why should the moon be dazzling bright?
My lover's call I seem to hear;
To the air I reply, "Yes, dear!"

---

[1] It was said that Midnight Songs were written by a Southern woman,
including the lowing songs.

SPRING SONG

How vernal flowers fascinate!
How vernal birds sing desolate!
How vernal wind brings love to my heart!
It blows my silken skirt apart.

SUMMER SONG

Green lotus leaves on water spread.
How bright are lotus blossoms red!
My lover longs to pluck me off;[1]
I yearn for lotus seed of love.

---

[1] The Southern women compares herself to a lotus blossom.

AUTUMN SONG

With windows open to cool breeze,
Neath slanting moon we sleep with ease.
At midnight no voice has left traces;
In curtained bed two smiling faces.

WINTER SONG

Three-foot-thick ice on the pond piles;
White snow outspreads for miles and miles.
My love for you lasts like green pine.
Will your love for me last like mine?

SONG OF THE WESTERN ISLET

In dream I see mume blossoms snowing;
To Western Isle again I'm going.
I'll send a sprig to northern shore
For my beloved I see no more.
In apricot-yellow silk dress,
E'en blackbirds envy my dark tress.
Where is the Western Islet? Where?
I row across the bridge o'er there
Only to find shrikes wheeling low
And through the trees at dusk winds blow.
Beneath the trees, inside the gate,
My hair adorned, I come to wait.
My lover comes not to my bower;
I go to gather lotus flower.
In south pool I pluck lotus red,
Which grows e'en high above my head.
I bow and pick up its love-seed
So green that water can't exceed.
I put the love-seed in one sleeve,
Red at the core as I perceive.
He never comes; I'm ill at ease
And watch for message-bearing geese.

The wild geese are mute as the flower;

I go on top of the blue tower.

To bring him within sight it fails;

All day long I stop at the rails.

In vain I lean on balustrade,

Letting fall my hands white like jade.

I see as I roll up the screen

The sky and waves in vain are green.

I dream as dreams the boundless sea.

From grief nor he nor I am free.

Should south wind know what's in my breast,

It would blow my dream to Islet West.

Song of MuLan

Alack, alas! alack, alas!
She weaves and sees the shuttle pass.
You cannot hear the shuttle, why?
Its whir is drowned in her deep sigh.
"Oh, what are you thinking about?
Will you tell us? Will you speak out?"
"I have no worry on my mind,
Nor have I grief of any kind.
I read the battleroll last night;
The Khan has ordered men to fight.
The roll was written in twelve books;
My father's name was in the nooks.
My father has no grown-up son,
For elder brother I have none.
I'll buy a horse of hardy race
And serve in my old father's place."

She buys at the fair east and west
A steed with saddle fitting best;
She buys a long whip north and south
And metal bit for the horse's mouth.
At dawn she leaves her parents by the city wall;
At dusk she reaches Yellow River shore.

All night she listens for old folk's familiar call,
But only hears the Yellow River's roar.
At dawn she leaves the Yellow River shore;
To Mountains Black she goes her way.
At night she hears old folk's familiar voice no more,
But only on north mountains Tartar horses neigh.

For miles and miles the army march along
And cross the mountain barriers as in flight.
The northern wind has chilled the watchmen's gong,
Their coat of mail glistens in wintry light.
In ten years they've lost many captains strong,
But battle-hardened warriors come back in delight.

Back, they have their audience with the Khan in the hall,
Honors and gifts are lavished on them with grace.
The Khan asks her what she wants after all.
"A camel fleet to carry me to my native place."

Hearing that she has come, and leaning on each other,
Her parents come to meet her at the city gate.
Her sister rouges her face and her younger brother,
Sharpening knife, kills pig and sheep to celebrate.
She opens the doors east and west

And sits on her bed for a rest.
She doffs her garb worn under fire
And wears again female attire.
Before the window she arranges her hair
And in the mirror sees her image fair.
Then she comes out to see her former mate,
Who stares at her in amazement great;
"We have marched together for twelve years,
But did not know there was a lass 'mid our compeers!"

Both buck and doe have lilting gait
And both their eyelids palpitate.
When side by side two rabbits go,
Who can tell the buck from the doe?

A SHEPHERD'S SONG

By the side of the rill,

At the foot of the hill,

The grassland stretches 'neath the firmament tranquil.

The boundless grassland lies

Beneath the boundless skies.

When the winds blow

And grass bends low,

My sheep and cattle will emerge before your eyes.

许译中国经典诗文集

汉魏六朝诗选

许渊冲　译

五洲传播出版社　中华书局

大风歌

大风起兮云飞扬，
威加海内兮归故乡。
安得猛士兮守四方！

垓下歌

力拔山兮气盖世，时不利兮骓不逝。
骓不逝兮可奈何，虞兮虞兮奈若何！

和项王歌

汉兵已略地，四方楚歌声。
大王意气尽，贱妾何聊生。

刘彻

秋风辞

秋风起兮白云飞，草木黄落兮雁南归。
兰有秀兮菊有芳，怀佳人兮不能忘。
泛楼船兮济汾河，横中流兮扬素波。
箫鼓鸣兮发棹歌，欢乐极兮哀情多。
少壮几时兮奈老何！

司马相如

琴歌

凤兮凤兮归故乡，遨游四海求其皇。
时未遇兮无所将，何悟今兮升斯堂！
有艳淑女在闺房，室迩人遐毒我肠。
何缘交颈为鸳鸯，胡颉颃兮共翱翔！

李延年

北方有佳人

北方有佳人，绝世而独立。
一顾倾人城，再顾倾人国。
宁不知倾城与倾国？佳人难再得！

怨歌行

新裂齐纨素，鲜洁如霜雪，
裁为合欢扇，团团似明月。
出入君怀袖，动摇微风发。
常恐秋节至，凉飙夺炎热，
弃捐箧笥中，恩情中道绝。

羽林郎

昔有霍家奴，姓冯名子都。
依倚将军势，调笑酒家胡。
胡姬年十五，春日独当炉。
长裾连理带，广袖合欢襦。
头上蓝田玉，耳后大秦珠。
两鬟何窈窕，一世良所无。
一鬟五百万，两鬟千万余。
"不意金吾子，娉婷过我庐。
银鞍何煜爚，翠盖空踟蹰。
就我求清酒，丝绳提玉壶；
就我求珍肴，金盘脍鲤鱼。
贻我青铜镜，结我红罗裾。
不惜红罗裂，何论轻贱躯！
男儿爱后妇，女子重前夫。
人生有新故，贵贱不相逾。
多谢金吾子，私爱徒区区。"

苏武

苏武诗四首

其三

结发为夫妻，恩爱两不疑。

欢娱在今夕，嬿婉及良时。

征夫怀远路，起视夜何其？

参辰皆已没，去去从此辞。

行役在战场，相见未有期。

握手一长叹，泪为生别滋。

努力爱春华，莫忘欢乐时。

生当复来归，死当长相思。

无名氏

战城南

战城南，死郭北，野死不葬乌可食。

为我谓乌："且为客豪，

野死谅不葬，腐肉安能去子逃？"

水深激激，蒲苇冥冥。

枭骑战斗死，驽马徘徊鸣。

梁筑室，何以南，何以北，

禾黍不获君何食？愿为忠臣安可得？

思子良臣，良臣诚可思。

朝行出攻，莫不夜归。

有所思

有所思，乃在大海南。
何用问遗君？双珠玳瑁簪，用玉绍缭之。
闻君有他心，拉杂摧烧之。
摧烧之，当风扬其灰。
从今以往，勿复相思！相思与君绝！
鸡鸣狗吠，兄嫂当知之。
妃呼豨！秋风肃肃晨风飔，东方须臾高知之。

上邪

上邪！我欲与君相知，长命无绝衰。
山无陵，江水为竭，冬雷震震，
夏雨雪，天地合，乃敢与君绝！

江南

江南可采莲，莲叶何田田。
鱼戏莲叶间。
鱼戏莲叶东，鱼戏莲叶西，
鱼戏莲叶南，鱼戏莲叶北。

平陵东

平陵东，松柏桐，不知何人劫义公。
劫义公，在高堂下，交钱百万两走马。
两走马，亦诚难，顾见追吏心中恻。
心中恻，血出漉，归告我家卖黄犊。

陌上桑

日出东南隅，照我秦氏楼。
秦氏有好女，自名为罗敷。
罗敷喜蚕桑，采桑城南隅。
青丝为笼系，桂枝为笼钩。
头上倭堕髻，耳中明月珠。
缃绮为下裙，紫绮为上襦。
行者见罗敷，下担捋髭须。
少年见罗敷，脱帽着帩头。
耕者忘其犁，锄者忘其锄。
来归相怒怨，但坐观罗敷。

使君从南来，五马立踟蹰。
使君遣吏往，"问是谁家姝。"
"秦氏有好女，自名为罗敷。"
"罗敷年几何？"
"二十尚不足，十五颇有余。"
"使君谢罗敷，宁可共载不？"

罗敷前置辞："使君一何愚！
使君自有妇，罗敷自有夫。

"东方千余骑，夫婿居上头。
何用识夫婿？白马从骊驹，
青丝系马尾，黄金络马头，
腰中鹿卢剑，可值千万余。
十五府小史，二十朝大夫，
三十侍中郎，四十专城居。
为人洁白皙，鬤鬤颇有须，
盈盈公府步，冉冉府中趋。
坐中数千人，皆言夫婿殊。"

长歌行

青青园中葵，朝露待日晞。
阳春布德泽，万物生光辉。
常恐秋节至，焜黄华叶衰。
百川东到海，何时复西归。
少壮不努力，老大徒伤悲。

东门行

出东门，不顾归；来入门，怅欲悲；
盎中无斗米储，还视架上无悬衣。
拔剑东门去，舍中儿母牵衣啼：
"他家但愿富贵，贱妾与君共铺糜。
上用仓浪天故，下当用此黄口儿，今非！"
"咄！行，吾去为迟！白发时下难久居。"

饮马长城窟行

青青河畔草，绵绵思远道。
远道不可思，宿昔梦见之。
梦见在我傍，忽觉在他乡。
他乡各异县，展转不相见。
枯桑知天风，海水知天寒。
入门各自媚，谁肯相为言！
客从远方来，遗我双鲤鱼。
呼儿烹鲤鱼，中有尺素书。
长跪读素书，书中竟何如？
上言加餐食，下言长相忆。

妇病行

妇病连年累岁，传呼丈人前一言。
当言未及得言，不知泪下一何翩翩。
属累君两三孤子，莫我儿饥且寒，
有过慎莫笪笞，行当折摇，思复念之！

乱曰：抱时无衣，襦复无里。
闭门塞牖，舍孤儿到市。
道逢亲交，泣坐不能起。
从乞求与孤买饵。
对交啼泣，泪不可止：
"我欲不伤悲不能已。"
探怀中钱持授交。
入门见孤儿，啼索其母抱。
徘徊空舍中，"行复尔耳！弃置勿复道"。

艳歌行

翩翩堂前燕，冬藏夏来见。
兄弟两三人，流宕在他县。
故衣谁当补？新衣谁当绽？
赖得贤主人，览取为吾绽。
夫婿从门来，斜柯西北眄。
"语卿且勿眄，水清石自见。"
石见何累累，远行不如归。

白头吟

皑如山上雪，皎若云间月。
闻君有两意，故来相决绝。
今日斗酒会，明旦沟水头。
躞蹀御沟上，沟水东西流。
凄凄复凄凄，嫁娶不须啼。
愿得一心人，白头不相离。
竹竿何袅袅，鱼尾何簁簁。
男儿重意气，何用钱刀为。

蜨蝶行

蜨蝶之遨游东园，
奈何卒逢三月养子燕，接我苜蓿间。
持之我入紫深宫中，行缠之傅欂栌间，
雀来燕。
燕子见衔哺来，摇头鼓翼何轩奴轩！

乌生八九子

乌生八九子，端坐秦氏桂树间。唶我！
秦氏家有游遨荡子，工用睢阳强，苏合弹。
左手持强弹两丸，出入乌东西。唶我！
一丸即发中乌身，乌死魂魄飞扬上天。
阿母生乌子时，乃在南山岩石间。唶我！
人民安知乌子处？蹊径窈窕安从通？
白鹿乃在上林西苑中，射工尚复得白鹿脯。唶我！
黄鹄摩天极高飞，后宫尚复得烹煮之。
鲤鱼乃在洛水深渊中，钓竿尚得鲤鱼口。唶我！
人民生，各各有寿命，死生何须复道前后！

枯鱼过河泣

枯鱼过河泣，何时悔复及！
作书与鲂鲕，相教慎出入。

悲歌

悲歌可以当泣，远望可以当归。
思念故乡，郁郁累累。
欲归家无人，欲渡河无船。
心思不能言，肠中车轮转。

孔雀东南飞

序曰：汉末建安中，庐江府小吏焦仲卿妻刘氏，为
仲卿母所遣，自誓不嫁。其家逼之，乃投水而死。
仲卿闻之，亦自缢于庭树。时人伤之，为诗云尔。

孔雀东南飞，五里一徘徊。
"十三能织素，十四学裁衣，
十五弹箜篌，十六诵诗书。
十七为君妇，心中常苦悲。
君既为府吏，守节情不移，
贱妾留空房，相见常日稀。
鸡鸣入机织，夜夜不得息。
三日断五匹，大人故嫌迟。
非为织作迟，君家妇难为！

妾不堪驱使，徒留无所施，
便可白公姥，及时相遣归。”

府吏得闻之，堂上启阿母：
“儿已薄禄相，幸复得此妇，
结发同枕席，黄泉共为友。
共事二三年，始尔未为久，
女行无偏斜，何意致不厚？”
阿母谓府吏：“何乃太区区！
此妇无礼节，举动自专由。
吾意久怀忿，汝岂得自由！
东家有贤女，自名秦罗敷，
可怜体无比，阿母为汝求。
便可速遣之，遣去慎莫留！”
府吏长跪告，伏惟启阿母：
“今若遣此妇，终老不复取！”
阿母得闻之，槌床便大怒：
“小子无所畏，何敢助妇语！
吾已失恩义，会不相从许！”

府吏默无声，再拜还入户，
举言谓新妇，哽咽不能语：
“我自不驱卿，逼迫有阿母。
卿但暂还家，吾今且报府。
不久当归还，还必相迎取。
以此下心意，慎勿违吾语。”

新妇谓府吏："勿复重纷纭！
往昔初阳岁，谢家来贵门。
奉事循公姥，进止敢自专？
昼夜勤作息，伶俜萦苦辛。
谓言无罪过，供养卒大恩；
仍更被驱遣，何言复来还？
妾有绣腰襦，葳蕤自生光；
红罗复斗帐，四角垂香囊；
箱帘六七十，绿碧青丝绳，
物物各自异，种种在其中。
人贱物亦鄙，不足迎后人，
留待作遗施，于今无会因。
时时为安慰，久久莫相忘！"

鸡鸣外欲曙，新妇起严妆。
著我绣夹裙，事事四五通。
足下蹑丝履，头上玳瑁光。
腰若流纨素，耳着明月珰。
指如削葱根，口如含朱丹。
纤纤作细步，精妙世无双。
上堂拜阿母，阿母怒不止。
"昔作女儿时，生小出野里，
本自无教训，兼愧贵家子。
受母钱帛多，不堪母驱使。
今日还家去，念母劳家里。"
却与小姑别，泪落连珠子。

"新妇初来时，小姑始扶床；
今日被驱遣，小姑如我长。
勤心养公姥，好自相扶将。
初七及下九，嬉戏莫相忘。"
出门登车去，涕落百余行。

府吏马在前，新妇车在后，
隐隐何甸甸，俱会大道口。
下马入车中，低头共耳语：
"誓不相隔卿，且暂还家去；
吾今且赴府，不久当还归。
誓天不相负！"
新妇谓府吏："感君区区怀！
君既若见录，不久望君来。
君当作磐石，妾当作蒲苇，
蒲苇纫如丝，磐石无转移。
我有亲父兄，性行暴如雷，
恐不任我意，逆以煎我怀。"
举手长劳劳，二情同依依。

入门上家堂，进退无颜仪。
阿母大拊掌："不图子自归，
十三教汝织，十四能裁衣，
十五弹箜篌，十六知礼仪，
十七遣汝嫁，谓言无誓违。
汝今何罪过，不迎而自归？"
兰芝惭阿母："儿实无罪过。"

阿母大悲摧。

还家十余日，县令遣媒来。
云有第三郎，窈窕世无双。
年始十八九，便言多令才。
阿母谓阿女："汝可去应之。"
阿女含泪答："兰芝初还时，
府吏见丁宁，结誓不别离。
今日违情义，恐此事非奇。
自可断来信，徐徐更谓之。"
阿母白媒人：
"贫贱有此女，始适还家门。
不堪吏人妇，岂合令郎君？
幸可广问讯，不得便相许。"

媒人去数日，寻遣丞请还，
说有兰家女，承籍有宦官。
云有第五郎，娇逸未有婚。
遣丞为媒人，主簿通语言。
直说太守家，有此令郎君，
既欲结大义，故遣来贵门。
阿母谢媒人：
"女子先有誓，老姥岂敢言！"
阿兄得闻之，怅然心中烦。
举言谓阿妹："作计何不量！
先嫁得府吏，后嫁得郎君，
否泰如天地，足以荣汝身。

不嫁义郎体，其往欲何云？"
兰芝仰头答："理实如兄言。
谢家事夫婿，中道还兄门。
处分适兄意，那得自任专？
虽与府吏要，渠会永无缘。
登即相许和，便可作婚姻。"
媒人下床去，诺诺复尔尔。
还部白府君："下官奉使命，
言谈大有缘。"府君得闻之，
心中大欢喜。视历复开书，
便利此月内，六合正相应。
"良吉三十日，今已二十七，
卿可去成婚。"交语速装束，
络绎如浮云。青雀白鹄舫，
四角龙子幡，婀娜随风转。
金车玉作轮，踯躅青骢马，
流苏金镂鞍。
赍钱三百万，皆用青丝穿。
杂彩三百匹，交广市鲑珍。
从人四五百，郁郁登郡门。

阿母谓阿女：
"适得府君书，明日来迎汝。
何不作衣裳？莫令事不举！"
阿女默无声，手巾掩口啼，
泪落便如泻。

移我琉璃榻，出置前窗下。
左手持刀尺，右手执绫罗。
朝成绣夹裙，晚成单罗衫。
晻晻日欲暝，愁思出门啼。
府吏闻此变，因求假暂归。
未至二三里，摧藏马悲哀。
新妇识马声，蹑履相逢迎。
怅然遥相望，知是故人来。
举手拍马鞍，嗟叹使心伤：
"自君别我后，人事不可量。
果不如先愿，又非君所详。
我有亲父母，逼迫兼弟兄，
以我应他人，君还何所望！"
府吏谓新妇："贺卿得高迁！
磐石方且厚，可以卒千年；
蒲苇一时纫，便作旦夕间。
卿当日胜贵，吾独向黄泉！"
新妇谓府吏："何意出此言！
同是被逼迫，君尔妾亦然。
黄泉下相见，勿违今日言！"
执手分道去，各各还家门。
生人作死别，恨恨那可论！
念与世间辞，千万不复全。

府吏还家去，上堂拜阿母：
"今日大风寒，寒风摧树木，

严霜结庭兰。

儿今日冥冥，令母在后单。
故作不良计，勿复怨鬼神！
命如南山石，四体康且直！”
阿母得闻之，零泪应声落：
“汝是大家子，仕宦于台阁。
慎勿为妇死，贵贱情何薄？
东家有贤女，窈窕艳城郭，
阿母为汝求，便复在旦夕。”
府吏再拜还，长叹空房中，
作计乃尔立。
转头向户里，渐见愁煎迫。

其日牛马嘶，新妇入青庐。
庵庵黄昏后，寂寂人定初。
“我命绝今日，魂去尸长留！”
揽裙脱丝履，举身赴清池。
府吏闻此事，心知长别离。
徘徊庭树下，自挂东南枝。

两家求合葬，合葬华山傍。
东西植松柏，左右种梧桐。
枝枝相覆盖，叶叶相交通，
中有双飞鸟，自名为鸳鸯。
仰头相向鸣，夜夜达五更。
行人驻足听，寡妇起彷徨。
多谢后世人，戒之慎勿忘！

古诗十九首

行行重行行

行行重行行，与君生别离。
相去万余里，各在天一涯。
道路阻且长，会面安可知？
胡马依北风，越鸟巢南枝。
相去日已远，衣带日已缓。
浮云蔽白日，游子不顾返。
思君令人老，岁月忽已晚。
弃捐勿复道，努力加餐饭。

青青河畔草

青青河畔草，郁郁园中柳。
盈盈楼上女，皎皎当窗牖。
娥娥红粉妆，纤纤出素手。
昔为倡家女，今为荡子妇。
荡子行不归，空床难独守。

青青陵上柏

青青陵上柏，磊磊涧中石。
人生天地间，忽如远行客。
斗酒相娱乐，聊厚不为薄。
驱车策驽马，游戏宛与洛。
洛中何郁郁，冠带自相索。
长衢罗夹巷，王侯多第宅。
两宫遥相望，双阙百余尺。
极宴娱心意，戚戚何所迫？

今日良宴会

今日良宴会，欢乐难具陈。
弹筝奋逸响，新声妙入神。
令德唱高言，识曲听其真。
齐心同所愿，含意俱未伸。
人生寄一世，奄忽若飙尘。
何不策高足，先踞要路津？
无为守贫贱，轗轲常苦辛。

西北有高楼

西北有高楼，上与浮云齐。
交疏结绮窗，阿阁三重阶。
上有弦歌声，音响一何悲！
谁能为此曲？无乃杞梁妻。
清商随风发，中曲正徘徊。
一弹再三叹，慷慨有余哀。
不惜歌者苦，但伤知音稀。
愿为双鸿鹄，奋翅起高飞。

涉江采芙蓉

涉江采芙蓉，兰泽多芳草。
采之欲遗谁？所思在远道。
还顾望旧乡，长路漫浩浩。
同心而离居，忧伤以终老。

明月皎夜光

明月皎夜光，促织鸣东壁。
玉衡指孟冬，众星何历历。
白露沾野草，时节忽复易。
秋蝉鸣树间，玄鸟逝安适？
昔我同门友，高举振六翮。
不念携手好，弃我如遗迹。
南箕北有斗，牵牛不负轭。
良无盘石固，虚名复何益？

冉冉孤生竹

冉冉孤生竹，结根泰山阿。
与君为新婚，菟丝附女萝。
菟丝生有时，夫妇会有宜。
千里远结婚，悠悠隔山陂。
思君令人老，轩车来何迟。
伤彼蕙兰花，含英扬光辉，
过时而不采，将随秋草萎。
君亮执高节，贱妾亦何为？

庭中有奇树

庭中有奇树，绿叶发华滋。
攀条折其荣，将以遗所思。
馨香盈怀袖，路远莫致之。
此物何足贡？但感别经时。

迢迢牵牛星

迢迢牵牛星，皎皎河汉女。
纤纤擢素手，札札弄机杼。
终日不成章，泣涕零如雨。
河汉清且浅，相去复几许？
盈盈一水间，脉脉不得语。

回车驾言迈

回车驾言迈，悠悠涉长道。
四顾何茫茫，东风摇百草。
所遇无故物，焉得不速老？
盛衰各有时，立身苦不早。
人生非金石，岂能长寿考？
奄忽随物化，荣名以为宝。

东城高且长

东城高且长，逶迤自相属。
回风动地起，秋草萋已绿。
四时更变化，岁暮一何速。
晨风怀苦心，蟋蟀伤局促。
荡涤放情志，何为自结束？
燕赵多佳人，美者颜如玉。
被服罗裳衣，当户理清曲。
音响一何悲，弦急知柱促。
驰情整中带，沉吟聊踟蹰。
思为双飞燕，衔泥巢君屋。

驱车上东门

驱车上东门，遥望郭北墓。
白杨何萧萧，松柏夹广路。
下有陈死人，杳杳即长暮。
潜寐黄泉下，千载永不寤。
浩浩阴阳移，年命如朝露。
人生忽如寄，寿无金石固。
万岁更相送，贤圣莫能度。
服食求神仙，多为药所误。
不如饮美酒，被服纨与素。

去者日以疏

去者日以疏，来者日以亲。
出郭门直视，但见丘与坟。
古墓犁为田，松柏摧为薪。
白杨多悲风，萧萧愁杀人。
思还故里闾，欲归道无因。

生年不满百

生年不满百，常怀千岁忧。
昼短苦夜长，何不秉烛游？
为乐当及时，何能待来兹？
愚者爱惜费，但为后世嗤。
仙人王子乔，难可与等期。

凛凛岁云暮

凛凛岁云暮，蟋蟀夕鸣悲。
凉风率已厉，游子寒无衣。
锦衾遗洛浦，同袍与我违。
独宿累长夜，梦想见容辉。
良人惟古欢，枉驾惠前绥。
"愿得常巧笑，携手同车归。"
既来不须臾，又不处重闱。
亮无晨风翼，焉能凌风飞？
眄睐以适意，引领遥相睎。
徙倚怀感伤，垂涕沾双扉。

孟冬寒气至

孟冬寒气至，北风何惨慄。
愁多知夜长，仰观众星列。
三五明月满，四五蟾兔缺。
客从远方来，遗我一书札。
上言长相思，下言久离别。
置书怀袖中，三岁字不灭。
一心抱区区，惧君不识察。

客从远方来

客从远方来，遗我一端绮。
相去万余里，故人心尚尔。
文采双鸳鸯，裁为合欢被。
著以长相思，缘以结不解。
以胶投漆中，谁能别离此。

明月何皎皎

明月何皎皎，照我罗床帏。
忧愁不能寐，揽衣起徘徊。
客行虽云乐，不如早旋归。
出户独彷徨，愁思当告谁。
引领还入房，泪下沾裳衣。

上山采蘼芜

上山采蘼芜，下山逢故夫。
长跪问故夫："新人复何如？"
"新人虽言好，未若故人姝。
颜色类相似，手爪不相如。"
"新人从门入，故人从阁去。"
"新人工织缣，故人工织素。
织缣日一匹，织素五丈余，
将缣来比素，新人不如故。"

步出城东门

步出城东门，遥望江南路。
前日风雪中，故人从此去。
我欲渡河水，河水深无梁。
愿为双黄鹄，高飞还故乡。

十五从军征

十五从军征，八十始得归。
道逢乡里人："家中有阿谁？"
"遥望是君家，"松柏冢累累。
兔从狗窦入，雉从梁上飞。
中庭生旅谷。井上生旅葵。
烹谷持作饭，采葵持作羹。
羹饭一时熟，不知贻阿谁。
出门东向望。泪落沾我衣。

悲愤诗

汉季失权柄，董卓乱天常。

志欲图篡弑，先害诸贤良。

逼迫迁旧邦，拥主以自强。

海内兴义师，欲共讨不祥。

卓众来东下，金甲耀日光。

平土人脆弱，来兵皆胡羌。

猎野围城邑，所向悉破亡。

斩截无孑遗，尸骸相撑拒。

马边悬男头，马后载妇女。

长驱西入关，迥路险且阻。

还顾邈冥冥，肝脾为烂腐。

所略有万计，不得令屯聚。

或有骨肉俱，欲言不敢语。

失意几微间，"辄言弊降虏。

要当以亭刃，我曹不活汝。"

岂敢惜性命？不堪其詈骂。

或便加棰杖，毒痛参并下。

旦则号泣行，夜则悲吟坐。

欲死不能得，欲生无一可。

彼苍者何辜？乃遭此厄祸。

边荒与华异，人俗少义理。

处所多霜雪，胡风春夏起。

翩翩吹我衣，肃肃入我耳。

感时念父母，哀叹无穷己，
有客从外来，闻之常欢喜，
迎问其消息，辄复非乡里。
邂逅徼时愿，骨肉来迎己。
己得自解免，当复弃儿子。
天属缀人心，念别无会期。
存亡永乖隔，不忍与之辞。
儿前抱我颈，问"母欲何之？
人言母当去，岂复有还时？
阿母常仁恻，今何更不慈？
我尚未成人，奈何不顾思！"
见此崩五内，恍惚生狂痴。
号泣手抚摩，当发复回疑。
兼有同时辈，相送告离别。
慕我独得归，哀叫声摧裂。
马为立踟蹰，车为不转辙。
观者皆歔欷，行路亦呜咽。

去去割情恋，遄征日遐迈。
悠悠三千里，何时复交会？
念我出腹子，胸臆为摧败。
既至家人尽，又复无中外。
城郭为山林，庭宇生荆艾。
白骨不知谁，纵横莫覆盖。

出门无人声，豺狼号且吠。
茕茕对孤景，怛咤糜肝肺。
登高远眺望，神魂忽飞驰。
奄若寿命尽，旁人相宽大。
为复强视息，虽生何聊赖？
托命于新人，竭心自勖厉。
流离成鄙贱，常恐复捐废，
人生几何时？怀忧终年岁。

蒿里行

关东有义士，兴兵讨群凶。
初期会盟津，乃心在咸阳。
军合力不齐，踌躇而雁行。
势利使人争，嗣还自相戕。
淮南弟称号，刻玺于北方。
铠甲生虮虱，万姓以死亡。
白骨露于野，千里无鸡鸣。
生民百遗一，念之断人肠。

短歌行

对酒当歌，人生几何？
譬如朝露，去日苦多。
慨当以慷，忧思难忘。
何以解忧？惟有杜康。
青青子衿，悠悠我心。
但为君故，沉吟至今。
呦呦鹿鸣，食野之苹。
我有嘉宾，鼓瑟吹笙。
明明如月，何时可掇？
忧从中来，不可断绝。
越陌度阡，枉用相存。
契阔谈宴，心念旧恩。
月明星稀，乌鹊南飞。
绕树三匝，何枝可依？
山不厌高，海不厌深。
周公吐哺，天下归心。

苦寒行

北上太行山，艰哉何巍巍！
羊肠坂诘屈，车轮为之摧。
树木何萧瑟！北风声正悲。
熊罴对我蹲，虎豹夹路啼。
谿谷少人民，雪落何霏霏！
延颈长叹息，远行多所怀。
我心何怫郁，思欲一东归。
水深桥梁绝，中路正徘徊。
迷惑失故路，薄暮无宿栖。
行行日已远，人马同时饥。
担囊行取薪，斧冰持作糜。
悲彼《东山》诗，悠悠使我哀。

观沧海

东临碣石，以观沧海。
水何澹澹，山岛竦峙。
树木丛生，百草丰茂。
秋风萧瑟，洪波涌起。
日月之行，若出其中；
星汉灿烂，若出其里。
幸甚至哉，歌以咏志。

龟虽寿

神龟虽寿，犹有竟时。

螣蛇乘雾，终为土灰。

老骥伏枥，志在千里；

烈士暮年，壮心不已。

盈缩之期，不但在天；

养怡之福，可得永年。

幸甚至哉，歌以咏志。

王粲

七哀诗

西京乱无象，豺虎方遘患。

复弃中国去，委身适荆蛮。

亲戚对我悲，朋友相追攀。

出门无所见，白骨蔽平原。

路有饥妇人，抱子弃草间。

顾闻号泣声，挥涕独不还。

"未知身死处，何能两相完？"

驱马弃之去，不忍听此言。

南登霸陵岸，回首望长安。

悟彼下泉人，喟然伤心肝。

七哀诗

其二

荆蛮非我乡，何为久滞淫？
方舟泝大江，日暮愁我心。
山冈有余映，岩阿增重阴。
狐狸驰赴穴，飞鸟翔故林。
流波激清响，猴猿临岸吟，
迅风拂裳袂，白露沾衣襟。
独夜不能寐，摄衣起抚琴。
丝桐感人情，为我发悲音。
羁旅无终极，忧思壮难任。

从军行

从军征遐路，讨彼东南夷。
方舟顺广川，薄暮未安坻。
白日半西山，桑梓有余晖。
蟋蟀夹岸鸣，孤鸟翩翩飞。
征夫心多怀，恻怆令吾悲。
下船登高防，草露沾我衣。
回身赴床寝，此愁当告谁？
身服干戈事，岂得念所私？
即戎有授命，兹理不可违。

陈琳

饮马长城窟行

饮马长城窟，水寒伤马骨。

往谓长城吏："慎莫稽留太原卒！"

"官作自有程，举筑谐汝声！"

"男儿宁当格斗死，何能怫郁筑长城？"

长城何连连，连连三千里。

边城多健少，内舍多寡妇。

作书与内舍："便嫁莫留住！

善侍新姑嫜，时时念我故夫子！"

报书往边地："君今出语一何鄙？"

"身在祸难中，何为稽留他家子？

生男慎莫举，生女哺用脯。

君独不见长城下，死人骸骨相撑拄？"

"结发行事君，慊慊心意关，

明知边地苦，贱妾何能久自全？"

刘桢

赠从弟

亭亭山上松，瑟瑟谷中风。

风声一何盛，松枝一何劲。

冰霜正惨凄，终岁常端正。

岂不罹凝寒？松柏有本性。

室思

浮云何洋洋，愿因通我词。
飘飖不可寄，徙倚徒相思。
人离皆复会，君独无返期。
自君之出矣，明镜暗不治。
思君如流水，何有穷已时。

定情诗

我出东门游，邂逅承清尘。
思君即幽房，侍寝执衣巾。
时无桑中契，迫此路侧人。
我既媚君姿，君亦悦我颜。
何以致拳拳？绾臂双金环。
何以道殷勤？约指一双银。
何以致区区？耳中双明珠。
何以致叩叩？香囊系肘后。
何以致契阔？绕腕双跳脱。
何以结恩情？美玉缀罗缨。
何以结中心？素缕连双针。
何以结相于？金薄画搔头。
何以慰别离？耳后玳瑁钗。
何以答欢忻？纨素三条裙。

何以结愁悲？白绢双中衣。
与我期何所？乃期东山隅。
日旰兮不来，谷风吹我襦。
远望无所见，涕泣起踟蹰。
与我期何所？乃期山南阳。
日中兮不来，飘风吹我裳。
逍遥莫谁睹，望君愁我肠。
与我期何所？乃期西山侧。
日夕兮不来，踟蹰长叹息。
远望凉风至，俯仰正衣服。
与我期何所？乃期山北岑。
日暮兮不来，凄风吹我襟。
望君不能坐，悲苦愁我心。
爱身以何为，惜我华色时。
中情既款款，然后克密期。
褰衣蹑茂草，谓君不我欺。
厕此丑陋质，徙倚无所之。
自伤失所欲，泪下如连丝。

燕歌行

秋风萧瑟天气凉，草木摇落露为霜。
群燕辞归鹄南翔，念君客游多思肠。
慊慊思归恋故乡，君何淹留寄他方？
贱妾茕茕守空房，忧来思君不敢忘，
不觉泪下沾衣裳。
援琴鸣弦发清商，短歌微吟不能长。
明月皎皎照我床，星汉西流夜未央。
牵牛织女遥相望，尔独何辜限河梁。

芙蓉池作

乘辇夜行游，逍遥步西园。
双溪相溉灌，嘉木绕通川。
卑枝拂羽盖，修条摩苍天。
惊风扶轮毂，飞鸟翔我前。
丹霞夹明月，华星出云间。
上天垂光彩，五色一何鲜。
寿命非松乔，谁能得神仙？
遨游快心意，保己终百年。

杂诗

一

漫漫秋夜长，烈烈北风凉。
展转不能寐，披衣起彷徨。
彷徨忽已久，白露沾我裳。
俯视清水波，仰看明月光。
天汉回西流，三五正纵横。
草虫鸣何悲，孤雁独南翔。
郁郁多悲思，绵绵思故乡。
愿飞安得翼？欲济河无梁。
向风长叹息，断绝我中肠。

二

西北有浮云，亭亭如车盖。
惜哉时不遇，适与飘风会。
吹我东南行，行行至吴会，
吴会非我乡，安得久留滞？
弃置勿复陈，客子常畏人。

吁嗟篇

吁嗟此转蓬，居世何独然！
长去本根逝，宿夜无休闲。
东西经七陌，南北越九阡。
卒遇回风起，吹我入云间。
自谓终天路，忽然下沉泉。
惊飚接我出，故归彼中田。
当南而更北，谓东而反西。
宕宕当何依？忽亡而复存。
飘飘周八泽，连翩历五山。
流转无恒处，谁知吾苦艰？
愿为中林草，秋随野火燔。
糜灭岂不痛？愿与株荄连。

箜篌引

置酒高殿上，亲友从我游。
中厨办丰膳，烹羊宰肥牛。
秦筝何慷慨，齐瑟和且柔。
阳阿奏奇舞，京洛出名讴。
乐饮过三爵，缓带倾庶羞。
主称千金寿，宾奉万年酬。
久要不可忘，薄终义所尤。
谦谦君子德，磬折欲何求？
惊风飘白日，光景驰西流。
盛时不再来，百年忽我遒。
生存华屋处，零落归山丘。
先民谁不死，知命复何忧？

野田黄雀行

高树多悲风，海水扬其波。
利剑不在掌，结交何须多？
不见篱间雀，见鹞自投罗？
罗家得雀喜，少年见雀悲。
拔剑捎罗网，黄雀得飞飞。
飞飞摩苍天，来下谢少年。

名都篇

名都多妖女，京洛出少年。

宝剑直千金，被服丽且鲜。

斗鸡东郊道，走马长楸间。

驰骋未能半，双兔过我前。

揽弓捷鸣镝，长驱上南山。

左挽因右发，一纵两禽连。

余巧未及展，仰手接飞鸢。

观者咸称善，众工归我妍。

归来宴平乐，美酒斗十千。

脍鲤臇胎鰕，炮鳖炙熊蹯。

鸣俦啸匹侣，列坐竟长筵。

连翩击鞠壤，巧捷惟万端。

白日西南驰，光景不可攀。

云散还城邑，清晨复来还。

美女篇

美女妖且闲，采桑岐路间。
柔条纷冉冉，落叶何翩翩。
攘袖见素手，皓腕约金环。
头上金爵钗，腰佩翠琅玕。
明珠交玉体，珊瑚间木难。
罗衣何飘飘，轻裾随风还。
顾盼遗光彩，长啸气若兰。
行徒用息驾，休者以忘餐。
借问女安居，乃在城南端。
青楼临大路，高门结重关。
容华耀朝日，谁不希令颜？
媒氏何所营？玉帛不时安。
佳人慕高义，求贤良独难。
众人徒嗷嗷，安知彼所观？
盛年处房室，中夜起长叹。

白马篇

白马饰金羁，连翩西北驰。

借问谁家子，幽并游侠儿。

少小去乡邑，扬声沙漠垂。

宿昔秉良弓，楛矢何参差。

控弦破左的，右发摧月支。

仰手接飞猱，俯身散马蹄。

狡捷过猴猿，勇剽若豹螭。

边城多警急，胡虏数迁移。

羽檄从北来，厉马登高堤。

长驱蹈匈奴，左顾陵鲜卑。

弃身锋刃端，性命安可怀？

父母且不顾，何言子与妻？

名编壮士籍，不得中顾私。

捐躯赴国难，视死忽如归。

赠白马王彪

谒帝承明庐，逝将归旧疆。
清晨发皇邑，日夕过首阳。
伊洛广且深，欲济川无梁。
泛舟越洪涛，怨彼东路长。
顾瞻恋城阙，引领情内伤。

太谷何寥廓，山树郁苍苍。
霖雨泥我涂，流潦浩纵横。
中逵绝无轨，改辙登高冈。
修坂造云日，我马玄以黄。

玄黄犹能进，我思郁以纡。
郁纡将何念？亲爱在离居。
本图相与偕，中更不克俱。
鸱枭鸣衡轭，豺狼当路衢。
苍蝇间白黑，谗巧令亲疏。
欲还绝无蹊，揽辔止踟蹰。

踟蹰亦何留？相思无终极。
秋风发微凉，寒蝉鸣我侧。
原野何萧条，白日忽西匿。
归鸟赴乔林，翩翩厉羽翼。
孤兽走索群，衔草不遑食。
感物伤我怀，抚心长太息。

太息将何为？天命与我违。
奈何念同生，一往形不归。
孤魂翔故域，灵柩寄京师。
存者忽复过，亡没身自衰。
人生处一世，去若朝露晞。
年在桑榆间，影响不能追。
自顾非金石，咄唶令心悲。

心悲动我神，弃置莫复陈。
丈夫志四海，万里犹比邻。
恩爱苟不亏，在远分日亲。
何必同衾帱，然后展殷勤。
忧思成疾疢，无乃儿女仁。
仓卒骨肉情，能不怀苦辛？

苦辛何虑思？天命信可疑。
虚无求列仙，松子久吾欺。
变故在斯须，百年谁能持？
离别永无会，执手将何时？
王其爱玉体，俱享黄发期。
收泪即长路，援笔从此辞。

送应氏

步登北邙阪，遥望洛阳山。
洛阳何寂寞，宫室尽烧焚。
垣墙皆顿擗，荆棘上参天。
不见旧耆老，但睹新少年。
侧足无行径，荒畴不复田。
游子久不归，不识陌与阡。
中野何萧条，千里无人烟。
念我平常居，气结不能言。

杂诗

其四

南国有佳人，容华若桃李。
朝游江北岸，夕宿潇湘沚。
时俗薄朱颜，谁为发皓齿？
俯仰岁将暮，荣耀难久恃。

七哀

明月照高楼，流光正徘徊。
上有愁思妇，悲叹有余哀。
借问叹者谁，言是宕子妻。
君行逾十年，孤妾常独栖。
君若清路尘，妾若浊水泥。
浮沉各异势，会合何时谐？
愿为西南风，长逝入君怀。
君怀良不开，贱妾当何依？

七步诗

煮豆燃豆萁，豆在釜中泣。
本是同根生，相煎何太急？

嵇康

赠兄秀才入军

其九

良马既闲，丽服有晖。
左揽繁弱，右接忘归。
风驰电逝，蹑景追飞。
凌厉中原，顾盼生姿。

阮籍

咏怀诗

其一

夜中不能寐，起坐弹鸣琴。
薄帷鉴明月，清风吹我襟。
孤鸿号外野，翔鸟鸣北林。
徘徊将何见？忧思独伤心。

其三

嘉树下成蹊，东园桃与李。
秋风吹飞藿，零落从此始。
繁华有憔悴，堂上生荆杞。
驱马舍之去，去上西山趾。
一身不自保，何况恋妻子。
凝霜被野草，岁暮亦云已。

车遥遥篇

车遥遥兮马洋洋，追思君兮不可忘。
君安游兮西入秦，愿为影兮随君身。
君在阴兮影不见，君依光兮妾所愿。

情诗

其三

清风动帷帘，晨月照幽房。
佳人处遐远，兰室无容光。
襟怀拥虚景，轻衾覆空床。
居欢惜夜促，在戚怨宵长。
拊枕独啸叹，感慨心内伤。

其五

游目四野外，逍遥独延伫。
兰蕙缘清渠，繁华荫绿渚。
佳人不在兹，取此欲谁与？
巢居知风寒，穴处识阴雨。
不曾远别离，安知慕俦侣？

潘岳

悼亡诗

荏苒冬春谢，寒暑忽流易。
之子归穷泉，重壤永幽隔。
私怀谁克从？淹留亦何益。
僶俛恭朝命，回心反初役。
望庐思其人，入室想所历。
帏屏无仿佛，翰墨有余迹。
流芳未及歇，遗挂犹在壁。
怅恍如或存，回遑忡惊惕。
如彼翰林鸟，双栖一朝只；
如彼游川鱼，比目中路析。
春风缘隙来，晨霤承檐滴。
寝息何时忘，沉忧日盈积。
庶几有时衰，庄缶犹可击。

王明君辞

我本汉家子，将适单于庭。

辞诀未及终，前驱已抗旌。

仆御涕流离，辕马为悲鸣。

哀郁伤五内，泣泪沾朱缨。

行行日已远，遂造匈奴城。

延我于穹庐，加我阏氏名。

殊类非所安，虽贵非所荣。

父子见凌辱，对之惭且惊。

杀身良不易，默默以苟生。

苟生亦何聊，积思常愤盈。

愿假飞鸿翼，弃之以遐征。

飞鸿不我顾，伫立以屏营。

昔为匣中玉，今为粪上英。

朝华不足欢，甘与秋草并。

传语后世人，远嫁难为情。

陆机

赴洛道中作

远游越山川，山川修且广。
振策陟崇丘，案辔遵平莽。
夕息抱影寐，朝徂衔思往。
顿辔倚高岩，侧听悲风响。
清露坠素辉，明月一何朗。
抚枕不能寐，振衣独长想。

左思

咏史八首

其一

弱冠弄柔翰，卓荦观群书，
著论准《过秦》，作赋拟《子虚》。
边城苦鸣镝，羽檄飞京都。
虽非甲胄士，畴昔览穰苴。
长啸激清风，志若无东吴。
铅刀贵一割，梦想骋良图。
左眄澄江湘，右盼定羌胡。
功成不受爵，长揖归田庐。

其二

郁郁涧底松，离离山上苗。

以彼径寸茎，荫此百尺条。

世胄蹑高位，英俊沉下僚。

地势使之然，由来非一朝。

金张藉旧业，七叶珥汉貂。

冯公岂不伟，白首不见招。

张翰

思吴江歌

秋风起兮木叶飞，吴江水兮鲈正肥。

三千里兮家未归，恨难禁兮仰天悲。

张载

七哀诗

其一

北芒何垒垒，高陵有四五。

借问谁家坟，皆云汉世主。

恭文遥相望，原陵郁膴膴。

季世丧乱起，贼盗如豺虎。

毁坏过一抔，便房启幽户。

珠柙离玉体，珍宝见剽虏。

园寝化为墟，周墉无遗堵。

蒙茏荆棘生，蹊径登童竖。

狐兔窟其中，芜秽不复扫。

颓陇并垦发，萌隶营农圃。

昔为万乘君，今为丘中土。

感彼雍门言，凄怆哀今古。

盘中诗

山树高，鸟鸣悲。泉水深，鲤鱼肥。
空仓雀，常苦饥。吏人妇，会夫希。
出门望，见白衣。谓当是，而更非。
还入门，中心悲。北上堂，西入阶。
急机绞，杼声催。长叹息，当语谁。
君有行，妾念之。出有日，还无期。
结巾带，长相思。君忘妾，未知之。
妾忘君，罪当治。妾有行，宜知之。
黄者金，白者王。高者山，下者谷。
姓为苏，字伯玉，作人才多智谋足。
家居长安身在蜀，何惜马蹄归不数。
羊肉千斤酒百斛，令君马肥麦与粟。
今时人，智不足。与其书。不能读。
当从中央周四角。

刘琨

扶风歌

朝发广莫门，暮宿丹水山。
左手弯繁弱，右手挥龙渊。
顾瞻望宫阙，俯仰御飞轩。
据鞍长叹息，泪下如流泉。
系马长松下，发鞍高岳头。
烈烈悲风起，泠泠涧水流。
挥手长相谢，哽咽不能言。
浮云为我结，归鸟为我旋。
去家日已远，安知存与亡？
慷慨穷林中，抱膝独摧藏。
麋鹿游我前，猿猴戏我侧。
资粮既乏尽，薇蕨安可食？
揽辔命徒侣，吟啸绝岩中。
君子道微矣，夫子故有穷。
惟昔李骞期，寄在匈奴庭。
忠信反获罪，汉武不见明。
我欲竟此曲，此曲悲且长。
弃置勿重陈，重陈令心伤。

游仙诗

京华游侠窟，山林隐遁栖。
朱门何足荣？未若托蓬莱。
临源挹清波，陵冈掇丹荑。
灵谿可潜盘，安事登云梯？
漆园有傲吏，莱氏有逸妻。
进则保龙见，退为触藩羝。
高蹈风尘外，长揖谢夷齐。

兰亭诗

其三

三春启群品，寄畅在所因。
仰望碧天际，俯磐绿水滨。
寥朗无厓观，寓目理自陈。
大矣造化功，万殊莫不均。
群籁虽参差，适我无非新。

谢安 谢朗 谢道韫

咏雪联句

白雪纷纷何所似？谢安
撒盐空中差可拟。谢朗
未若柳絮因风起。谢道韫

顾恺之

神情诗

春水满四泽，夏云多奇峰。
秋月扬明辉，冬岭秀寒松。

时运

一

迈迈时运，穆穆良朝。
袭我春服，薄言东郊。
山涤余霭，宇暧微霄。
有风自南，翼彼新苗。

二

洋洋平泽，乃漱乃濯。
邈邈遐景，载欣载瞩。
人亦有言，称心易足。
挥兹一觞，陶然自乐。

三

延目中流，悠悠清沂。
童冠齐业，闲咏以归。
我爱其静，寤寐交挥。
但恨殊世，邈不可追。

四

斯晨斯夕，言息其庐。
花药分列，林竹翳如。
清琴横床，浊酒半壶，
黄唐莫逮，慨独在余。

游斜川

开岁倏五日，吾生行归休。
念之动中怀，及辰为兹游。
气和天惟澄，班坐依远流。
弱湍驰文鲂，闲谷矫鸣鸥。
迥泽散游目，缅然睇曾丘。
虽微九重秀，顾瞻无匹俦。
提壶接宾侣，引满更献酬。
未知从今去，当复如此否？
中觞纵遥情，忘彼千载忧。
且极今朝乐，明日非所求。

怨诗楚调示庞主簿邓治中

天道幽且远，鬼神茫昧然。
结发念善事，僶俛六九年。
弱冠逢世阻，始室丧其偏。
炎火屡焚如，螟蜮恣中田。
风雨纵横至，收敛不盈廛。
夏日长抱饥，寒夜无被眠。
造夕思鸡鸣，及晨愿乌迁。
在己何怨天，离忧凄目前。
吁嗟身后名，于我若浮烟，
慷慨独悲歌，钟期信为贤。

答庞参军

相知何必旧？倾盖定前言。
有客赏我趣，每每顾林园。
谈谐无俗调，所说圣人篇。
或有数斗酒，闲饮自欢然。
我实幽居士，无复东西缘。
物新人惟旧，弱毫多所宣。
情通万里外，形迹滞江山。
君其爱体素，来会在何年？

五月旦作和戴主簿

虚舟纵逸棹，回复遂无穷。
发岁始俯仰，星纪奄将中。
南窗罕时物，北林荣且丰。
神渊写时雨，晨色奏景风。
既来孰不去？人理固有终。
居常待其尽，曲肱岂伤冲？
迁化成夷险，肆志无窊隆。
即事如已高，何必升华嵩？

和刘柴桑

山泽久见招，胡事乃踌躇？
直为亲旧故，未忍言索居。
良辰入奇怀，挈杖还西庐。
荒途无归人，时时见废墟，
茅茨已就治，新畴复应畲。
谷风转凄薄，春醪解饥劬。
弱女虽非男，慰情良胜无。
栖栖世中事，岁月共相疏。
耕织称其用，过此奚所须？
去去百年外，身名同翳如。

酬刘柴桑

穷居寡人用，时忘四运周。
门庭多落叶，慨然已知秋。
新葵郁北牖，嘉穗养南畴。
今我不为乐，知有来岁不？
命室携童弱，良日登远游。

和郭主簿

其一

蔼蔼堂前林，中夏贮清阴。
凯风因时来，回飙开我襟。
息交游闲业，卧起弄书琴。
园蔬有余滋，旧谷犹储今。
营己良有极，过足非所钦。
春秫作美酒，酒熟吾自斟。
弱子戏我侧，学语未成音。
此事真复乐，聊用忘华簪。
遥遥望白云，怀古一何深！

其二

和泽周三春，清凉素秋节。
露凝无游氛，天高肃景澈。
陵岑耸逸峰，遥瞻皆奇绝。
芳菊开林耀，青松冠岩列。
怀此贞秀姿，卓为霜下杰。
衔觞念幽人，千载抚尔诀，
检素不获展，厌厌竟良月。

癸卯岁十二月中作与从弟敬远

寝迹衡门下，邈与世相绝。
顾盼莫谁知，荆扉昼常闭。
凄凄岁暮风，翳翳经日雪。
倾耳无希声，在目皓已洁。
劲气侵襟袖，箪瓢谢屡设。
萧索空宇中，了无一可悦。
历览千载书，时时见遗烈。
高操非所攀，谬得固穷节。
平津苟不由，栖迟讵为拙？
寄意一言外，兹契谁能别！

始作镇军参军经曲阿作

弱龄寄事外，委怀在琴书。
被褐欣自得，屡空常晏如。
时来苟冥会，宛辔憩通衢。
投策命晨装，暂与园田疏。
眇眇孤舟逝，绵绵归思纡。
我行岂不遥？登降千里余。
目倦川途异，心念山泽居。
望云惭高鸟，临水愧游鱼。
真想初在襟，谁谓形迹拘？
聊且凭化迁，终返班生庐。

乙巳岁三月为建威参军使都经钱溪

我不践斯境，岁月好已积。
晨夕看山川，事事悉如昔。
微雨洗高林，清飙矫云翮。
眷彼品物存，义风都未隔。
伊余何为者？勉励从兹役。
一形似有制，素襟不可易。
园田日梦想，安得久离析？
终怀在归舟，谅哉宜霜柏。

归去来兮辞

归去来兮，田园将芜胡不归？
既自以心为形役，奚惆怅而独悲！
悟以往之不谏，知来者之可追；
实迷途其未远，觉今是而昨非。
舟遥遥以轻飏，风飘飘而吹衣。
问征夫以前路，恨晨光之熹微。
乃瞻衡宇，载欣载奔。
僮仆欢迎，稚子候门。
三径就荒，松菊犹存。
携幼入室，有酒盈樽。
引壶觞以自酌，眄庭柯以怡颜。
倚南窗以寄傲，审容膝之易安。

园日涉以成趣，门虽设而常关。
策扶老以流憩，时矫首而遐观。
云无心以出岫，鸟倦飞而知还。
景翳翳以将入，抚孤松而盘桓。
归去来兮，请息交以绝游。
世与我而相违，复驾言兮焉求？
悦亲戚之情话，乐琴书以消忧。
农人告余以春及，将有事于西畴。
或命巾车，或棹孤舟。
既窈窕以寻壑，亦崎岖而经丘。
木欣欣以向荣，泉涓涓而始流。
善万物之得时，感吾生之行休。
已矣夫，
寓形于内能复几时，曷不委心任去留？
胡为乎遑遑欲何之？
富贵非吾愿，帝乡不可期。
怀良辰以孤往，或植杖而耘耔。
登东皋以舒啸，临清流而赋诗。
聊乘化以归尽，乐乎天命复奚疑！

形影神

形赠影

天地长不没，山川无改时。
草木得常理，霜露荣悴之。
谓人最灵智，独复不如兹。
适见在世中，奄去靡归期。
奚觉无一人，亲识岂相思？
但余平生物，举目情凄洏。
我无腾化术，必尔不复疑。
愿君取吾言，得酒莫苟辞！

影答形

存生不可言，卫生每苦拙。
诚愿游昆华，邈然兹道绝。
与子相遇来，未尝异悲悦。
憩荫若暂乖，止日终不别。
此同既难常，黯尔俱时灭。
身没名亦尽，念之五情热。
立善有遗爱，胡为不自竭？
酒云能消忧，方此讵不劣？

神释

大钧无私力，万理自森著。
人为三才中，岂不以我故？
与君虽异物，生而相依附。
结托既喜同，安得不相语？
三皇大圣人，今复在何处？
彭祖爱永年，欲留不得住。
老少同一死，贤愚无复数。
日醉或能忘，将非促龄具？
立善常所欣，谁当为汝誉？
甚念伤吾生，正宜委运去。
纵浪大化中，不喜亦不惧。
应尽便须尽，无复独多虑！

九日闲居

世短意常多，斯人乐久生。
日月依辰至，举俗爱其名。
露凄暄风急，气彻天象明。
往燕无遗影，来雁有余声。
酒能去百虑，菊能制颓龄。
如何蓬庐上，空视世运倾。
尘爵耻虚罍，寒华徒自荣。
敛襟独闲谣，缅焉起深情。
栖迟固多疑，淹留岂无成！

归园田居

其一

少无适俗韵，性本爱丘山。
误落尘网中，一去十三年，
羁鸟恋旧林，池鱼思故渊。
开荒南野际，守拙归园田。
方宅十余亩，草屋八九间。
榆柳荫后檐，桃李罗堂前。
暧暧远人村，依依墟里烟。
狗吠深巷中，鸡鸣桑树颠。
户庭无尘杂，虚室有余闲。
久在樊笼里，复得返自然。

其二

野外罕人事，穷巷寡轮鞅。
白日掩荆扉，虚室绝尘想。
时复墟里人，披草共来往。
相见无杂言，但道桑麻长。
桑麻日已长，我土日已广。
常恐霜霰至，零落同草莽。

其三

种豆南山下，草盛豆苗稀。
晨兴理荒秽，带月荷锄归，
道狭草木长，夕露沾我衣；
衣沾不足惜，但使愿无违。

其四

久去山泽游，浪莽林野娱。
试携子侄辈，披榛步荒墟。
徘徊丘垄间，依依昔人居。
井灶有遗处，桑竹残朽株。
借问采薪者，此人皆焉如？
薪者向我言：死没无复余。
一世异朝市，此语真不虚。
人生似幻化，终当归空无。

其五

怅恨独策还，崎岖历榛曲。
山涧清且浅，可以濯吾足。
漉我新熟酒，只鸡招近局。
日入室中暗，荆薪代明烛。
欢来苦夕短，已复至天旭。

乞食

饥来驱我去，不知竟何之！
行行至斯里，叩门拙言辞，
主人解余意，遗赠岂虚来？
谈话终日夕，觞至辄倾杯。
情欣新知欢，言咏遂赋诗，
感子漂母惠，愧我非韩才，
衔戢知何谢，冥报以相贻。

连雨独饮

运生会归尽，终古谓之然。
世间有松乔，于今定何间？
故老赠余酒，乃言饮得仙；
试酌百情远，重觞忽忘天。
天岂去此哉？任真无所先。
云鹤有奇翼，八表须臾还。
自我抱兹独，僶俛四十年。
形骸久已化，心在复何言！

移居

昔欲居南村，非为卜其宅。
闻多素心人，乐与数晨夕。
怀此颇有年，今日从兹役。
弊庐何必广，取足蔽床席。
邻曲时时来，抗言谈在昔。
奇文共欣赏，疑义相与析。

戊申岁六月中遇火

草庐寄穷巷，甘以辞华轩。
正夏长风急，林室顿烧燔。
一室无遗宇，舫舟荫门前。
迢迢新秋夕，亭亭月将圆。
果菜始复生，惊鸟尚未还。
中宵伫遥念，一盼周九天。
总发抱孤介，奄出四十年。
形迹凭化往，灵府常独闲。
贞刚自有质，玉石乃非坚。
仰想东户时，余粮宿中田。
鼓腹无所思，朝起暮归眠。
既已不遇兹，且遂灌我园。

饮酒

一

哀荣无定在，彼此更共之。
邵生瓜田中，宁似东陵时？
寒暑有代谢，人道每如兹。
达人解其会，逝将不复疑。
忽与一觞酒，日夕欢相持。

四

栖栖失林鸟，日暮犹独飞。
徘徊无定止，夜夜声转悲。
历响思清远，去来何所依？
因值孤生松，敛翮遥来归。
劲风无荣木，此荫独不衰。
托身已得所，千载不相违。

五

结庐在人境，而无车马喧。
问君何能尔，心远地自偏。
采菊东篱下，悠然见南山。
山气日夕佳，飞鸟相与还。
此中有真意，欲辩已忘言。

七

秋菊有佳色，挹露掇其英。
泛此忘忧物，远我遗世情。
一觞虽独进，杯尽壶自倾。
日入群动息，归鸟趋林鸣。
啸傲东轩下，聊复得此生。

八

青松在东园，众草没其姿。
凝霜殄异类，卓然见高枝。
连林人不觉，独树众乃奇。
提壶抚寒柯，远望时复为。
吾生梦幻间，何事绁尘羁！

九

清晨闻叩门，倒裳往自开。
问子为谁欤，田父有好怀。
壶浆远见候，疑我与时乖。
褴褛茅檐下，未足为高栖。
一世皆尚同，愿君汩其泥。
深感父老言，禀气寡所谐。
纡辔诚可学，违己岂非迷？
且共欢此饮，吾驾不可回。

十

在昔曾远游，直至东海隅。
道路迥且长，风波阻中途。
此行谁使然？似为饥所驱。
倾身营一饱，少许便有余。
恐此非名计，息驾归闲居。

十三

有客常同止，取舍邈异境。
一士长独醉，一夫终年醒。
醒醉还相笑，发言各不领。
规规一何愚？兀傲差若颖。
寄言酣中客，日没烛当秉。

十四

故人赏我趣，挈壶相与至。
班荆坐松下，数斟已复醉。
父老杂乱言，觞酌失行次。
不觉知有我，安知物为贵？
悠悠迷所留，酒中有深味。

十六

少年罕人事，游好在六经。
行行向不惑，淹留遂无成。
竞抱固穷节，饥寒饱所更。
弊庐交悲风，荒草没前庭。
披褐守长夜，晨鸡不肯鸣。
孟公不在兹，终以翳吾情。

十七

幽兰生前庭，含熏待清风。
清风脱然至，见别萧艾中。
行行失故路，任道或能通。
觉悟当念还，鸟尽废良弓。

十九

畴昔苦长饥，投耒去学仕。
将养不得节，冻绥固缠己。
是时向立年，志意多所耻。
遂尽介然分，终死归田里。
冉冉星气流，亭亭复一纪。
世路廓悠悠，杨朱所以止。
虽无挥金事，浊酒聊可恃。

二十

羲农去我久，举世少复真。
汲汲鲁中叟，弥缝使其淳。
凤鸟虽不至，礼乐暂得新。
洙泗辍微响，漂流逮狂秦。
诗书复何罪？一朝成灰尘。
区区诸老翁，为事诚殷勤。
如何绝世下，六籍无一亲？
终日驰车走，不见所问津，
若复不快饮，空负头上巾。
但恨多谬误，君当恕罪人。

止酒

居止次城邑，逍遥自闲止。
坐止高荫下，步止荜门里。
好味止园葵，大欢止稚子。
平生不止酒，止酒情无喜。
暮止不安寝，晨止不能起。
日日欲止之，营卫止不理。
徒知止不乐，未知止利己。
始觉止为善，今朝真止矣。
从此一止去，将止扶桑涘。
清颜止宿容，奚止千万祀！

责子

白发被两鬓，肌肤不复实。
虽有五男儿，总不好纸笔。
阿舒已二八，懒惰故无匹。
阿宣行志学，而不爱文术。
雍端年十三，不识六与七。
通子垂九龄，但觅梨与栗。
天运苟如此，且进杯中物。

拟古

其四

迢迢百尺楼，分明望四方。
暮作归云宅，朝为飞鸟堂。
山河满目中，平原独茫茫。
古时功名士，慷慨争此场；
一旦百岁后，相与还北邙。
松柏为人伐，高坟互低昂；
颓基无余主，游魂在何方？
荣华诚足贵，亦复可怜伤！

杂诗

一

人生无根蒂，飘如陌上尘。
分散逐风转，此已非常身。
落地为兄弟，何必骨肉亲？
得欢当作乐，斗酒聚比邻。
盛年不重来，一日难再晨；
及时当勉励，岁月不待人。

二

白日沦西阿，素月出东岭。
遥遥万里辉，荡荡空中景。
风来入房户，夜中枕席冷。
气变悟时易，不眠知夕永。
欲言无余和，挥杯劝孤影。
日月掷人去，有志不复骋。
念此怀悲凄，终晓不能静。

三

荣华难久居，盛衰不可量。
昔为三春蕖，今作秋莲房。
严霜结野草，枯悴未遽央。
日月还复周，我去不再阳。
眷眷往昔时，忆此断人肠。

四

丈夫志四海，我愿不知老。
亲戚共一处，子孙还相保。
觞弦肆朝日，樽中酒不燥。
缓带尽欢娱，起晚眠常早。
孰若当世士，冰炭满怀抱？
百年归丘垄，用此空名道！

五

忆我少壮时，无乐自欣豫。
猛志逸四海，骞翮思远翥。
荏苒岁月颓，此心稍已去；
值欢无复娱，每每多忧虑。
气力渐衰损，转觉日不如。
壑舟无须臾，引我不得住。
前途当几许？未知止泊处。
古人惜寸阴，念此使人惧。

六

昔闻长者言，掩耳每不喜。
奈何五十年，忽已亲此事。
求我盛年欢，一毫无复意。
去去转欲远，此生岂再值！
倾家持作乐，竟此岁月驶。
有子不留金，何用身后置！

七

日月不肯迟，四时相催迫。
寒风拂枯条，落叶掩长陌。
弱质与运颓，玄鬓早已白。
素标插人头，前途渐就窄。
家为逆旅舍，我如当去客。
去去欲何之？南山有旧宅。

八

代耕本非望，所业在田桑。
躬耕未曾替，寒馁常糟糠。
岂期过满腹？但愿饱粳粮。
御冬足大布，粗绨以应阳。
正尔不能得，哀哉亦可伤！
人皆尽获宜，拙生失其方。
理也可奈何，且为陶一觞。

咏贫士

万族各有托，孤云独无依。
暧暧空中灭，何时见余晖。
朝霞开宿雾，众鸟相与飞；
迟迟出林翮，未夕复来归。
量力守故辙，岂不寒与饥？
知音苟不存，已矣何所悲。

读《山海经》

孟夏草木长，绕屋树扶苏。
众鸟欣有托，吾亦爱吾庐。
既耕亦已种，时还读我书。
穷巷隔深辙，颇回故人车。
欢言酌春酒，摘我园中蔬。
微雨从东来，好风与之俱。
泛览周王传，流观山海图。
俯仰终宇宙，不乐复何如？

拟挽歌辞

有生必有死，早终非命促。
昨暮同为人，今旦在鬼录。
魂气散何之？枯形寄空木。
娇儿索父啼，良友抚我哭。
得失不复知，是非安能觉？
千秋万岁后，谁知荣与辱。
但恨在世时，饮酒不得足。

过始宁墅

束发怀耿介，逐物遂推迁。
违志似如昨，二纪及兹年。
缁磷谢清旷，疲苶惭贞坚。
拙疾相倚薄，还得静者便。
剖竹守沧海，任帆过旧山。
山行穷登顿，水涉尽洄沿。
岩峭岭稠叠，洲萦渚连绵。
白云抱幽石，绿篠媚清涟。
葺宇临回江，筑观基曾巅。
挥手告乡曲，三载期旋归，
且为树枌槚，无令孤愿言。

晚出西射堂

步出西城门，遥望城西岑。
连障叠巘崿，青翠杳深沉。
晓霜枫叶丹，夕曛岚气阴。
节往戚不浅，感来念已深，
羁雌恋旧侣，迷鸟怀故林。
含情尚劳爱，如何离赏心，
抚镜华缁鬓，揽带缓促衿。
安排徒空言，幽独赖鸣琴。

登池上楼

潜虬媚幽姿，飞鸿响远音。
薄霄愧云浮，栖川怍渊沉。
进德智所拙，退耕力不任。
徇禄反穷海，卧疴对空林。
衾枕昧节候，褰开暂窥临。
倾耳聆波澜，举目眺岖嵚。
初景革绪风，新阳改故阴。
池塘生春草，园柳变鸣禽。
祁祁伤豳歌，萋萋感楚吟。
索居易永久，离群难处心。
持操岂独古，无闷征在今。

登江中孤屿

江南倦历览，江北旷周旋。
怀新道转迥，寻异景不延。
乱流趋正绝，孤屿媚中川。
云日相辉映，空水共澄鲜。
表灵物莫赏，蕴真谁为传？
想象昆山姿，缅邈区中缘。
始信安期术，得尽养生年。

登上戍石鼓山

旅人心长久，忧忧自相接。
故乡路遥远，川陆不可涉。
汩汩莫与娱，发春托登蹑。
欢愿既无并，戚虑庶有协。
极目睐左阔，回顾眺右狭。
日没涧增波，云生岭逾叠。
白芷竞新苕，绿蘋齐初叶。
摘芳芳靡谖，愉乐乐不燮。
佳期缅无像，骋望谁云惬。

石壁精舍还湖中作

昏旦变气候，山水含清晖。
清晖能娱人，游子憺忘归。
出谷日尚早，入舟阳已微。
林壑敛暝色，云霞收夕霏。
芰荷迭映蔚，蒲稗相因依。
披拂趋南径，愉悦偃东扉。
虑澹物自轻，意惬理无违。
寄言摄生客，试用此道推。

从斤竹涧越岭溪行

猿鸣诚知曙，谷幽光未显。
岩下云方合，花上露犹泫。
逶迤傍隈隩，迢递陟陉岘。
过涧既厉急，登栈亦陵缅。
川渚屡径复，乘流玩回转。
蘋萍泛沉深，菰蒲冒清浅。
企石挹飞泉，攀林摘叶卷。
想见山阿人，薜萝若在眼。
握兰勤徒结，折麻心莫展。
情用赏为美，事昧竟谁辨？
观此遗物虑，一悟得所遣。

过白岸亭

拂衣遵沙垣，缓步入蓬屋。
近涧涓密石，远山映疏木。
空翠难强名，渔钓易为曲。
援萝临青崖，春心自相属。
交交止栩黄，呦呦食苹鹿。
伤彼人百哀，嘉尔承筐乐。
荣悴迭去来，穷通成休戚。
未若长疏散，万事恒抱朴。

石门岩上宿

朝搴苑中兰，畏彼霜下歇。
瞑还云际宿，弄此石上月。
鸟鸣识夜栖，木落知风发。
异音同至听，殊响俱清越。
妙物莫为赏，芳醑谁与伐？
美人竟不来，阳阿徒晞发。

入彭蠡湖口

客游倦水宿，风潮难俱论。
洲岛俱回合，圻岸屡崩奔，
乘月听哀狖，浥露馥芳荪。
春晚绿野秀，岩高白云屯。
千念集日夜，万感盈朝昏。
攀崖照石镜，牵叶入松门。
三江事多往，九派理空存。
灵物吝珍怪，异人秘精魂。
金膏灭明光，水碧辍流温。
徒作千里曲，弦绝念弥敦。

岁暮

殷忧不能寐，苦此夜难颓。
明月照积雪，朔风劲且哀。
运往无淹物，年逝觉易催。

东阳溪中赠答二首

一

可怜谁家妇，缘流洗素足。
明月在云间，迢迢不可得。

二

可怜谁家郎，缘流乘素舸。
但问情若为，月就云中堕。

代出自蓟北门行

羽檄起边亭，烽火入咸阳。

征骑屯广武，分兵救朔方。

严秋筋竿劲，虏阵精且强。

天子按剑怒，使者遥相望。

雁行缘石径，鱼贯度飞梁。

箫鼓流汉思，旌甲被胡霜。

疾风冲塞起，沙砾自飘扬。

马毛缩如蝟，角弓不可张。

时危见臣节，世乱识忠良。

投躯报明主，身死为国殇。

拟行路难

其四

泻水置平地，各自东西南北流。

人生亦有命，安能行叹复坐愁？

酌酒以自宽，举杯断绝歌路难。

心非木石岂无感？吞声踯躅不敢言。

梅花落

中庭杂树多，偏为梅咨嗟。
"问君何独然？""念其霜中能作花，
露中能作实，摇荡春风媚春日。
念尔零落逐寒风，徒有霜花无霜质！"

赠傅都曹别

轻鸿戏江潭，孤雁集洲沚。
邂逅两相亲，缘念共无已。
风雨好东西，一隔顿万里。
追忆栖宿时，声容满心耳。
落日川渚寒，愁云绕天起。
短翮不能翔，徘徊烟雾里。

谢朓

玉阶怨

夕殿下珠帘，流萤飞复息。
长夜缝罗衣，思君此何极？

王孙游

绿草蔓如丝，杂树红英发。
无论君不归，君归芳已歇。

游东田

戚戚苦无惊，携手共行乐。
寻云陟累榭，随山望菌阁。
远树暖阡阡，生烟纷漠漠。
鱼戏新荷动，鸟散余花落。
不对芳春酒，还望青山郭。

暂使下都夜发新林至京邑赠西府同僚

大江流日夜，客心悲未央。
徒念关山近，终知返路长。
秋河曙耿耿，寒渚夜苍苍。
引领见京室，宫雉正相望。
金波丽鳷鹊，玉绳低建章。
驱车鼎门外，思见昭丘阳。
驰晖不可接，何况隔两乡？
风云有鸟路，江汉限无梁。
常恐鹰隼击，时菊委严霜。
寄言蔚罗者，寥廓已高翔。

晚登三山还望京邑

灞涘望长安，河阳视京县。
白日丽飞甍，参差皆可见。
余霞散成绮，澄江静如练。
喧鸟覆春洲，杂英满芳甸。
去矣方滞淫，怀哉罢欢宴。
佳期怅何许，泪下如流霰。
有情知望乡，谁能鬓不变？

萧衍

子夜歌二首

一

恃爱如欲进，含羞未肯前。
朱口发艳歌，玉指弄娇弦。

二

朝日照绮窗，光风动纨罗。
巧笑蒨两犀，美目扬双蛾。

江南弄

众花杂色满上林，舒芳耀绿垂轻阴，
连手躞蹀舞春心。
舞春心，临岁腴。
中人望，独踟蹰。

范云

之零陵郡次新亭

江干远树浮，天末孤烟起。
江天自如合，烟树还相似。
沧流未可源，高飒去何已。

别诗

洛阳城东西，长作经时别。
昔去雪如花，今来花似雪。

江淹

古离别

远与君别者，乃至雁门关。
黄云蔽千里，游子何时还？
送君如昨日，檐前露已团。
不惜蕙草晚，所悲道里寒。
君在天一涯，妾身长别离。
愿一见颜色，不异琼树枝。
兔丝及水萍，所寄终不移。

沈约

临高台

高台不可望，望远使人愁。
连山无断绝，河水复悠悠。
所思竟何在，洛阳南陌头。
可望不可见，何用解人忧。

夜夜曲

河汉纵且横，北斗横复直。
星汉空如此，宁知心有忆？
孤灯暖不明，寒机晓犹织。
零泪向谁道，鸡鸣徒叹息。

咏湖中雁

白水满春塘，旅雁每回翔。
唼流牵弱藻，敛翮带余霜。
群浮动轻浪，单泛逐孤光。
悬飞竟不下，乱起未成行。
刷羽同摇漾，一举还故乡。

伤谢朓

吏部信才杰，文峰振奇响。
调与金石谐，思逐风云上。
岂言陵霜质，忽随人事往。
尺璧尔何冤，一旦同丘壤。

六忆诗四首

一

忆来时，灼灼上阶墀。
勤勤叙别离，慊慊道相思。
相看常不足，相见乃忘饥。

二

忆坐时，点点罗帐前。
或歌四五曲，或弄两三弦。
笑时应无比，嗔时更可怜。

三

忆食时，临盘动容色。
欲坐复羞坐，欲食复羞食。
含哺如不饥，擎瓯似无力。

四

忆眠时，人眠强未眠。
解罗不待劝，就枕更须牵。
复恐傍人见，娇羞在烛前。

柳恽

江南曲

汀洲采白蘋，日暖江南春。
洞庭有归客，潇湘逢故人。
故人何不返？春花复应晚。
不道新知乐，只言行路远。

酬范记室云

林密户稍阴，草滋阶欲暗。
风光蕊上轻，日色花中乱。
相思不独欢，伫立空为叹。
清谈莫共理，繁文徒可玩。
高唱子自轻，继音予可惮？

相送

客心已百念，孤游重千里。
江暗雨欲来，浪白风初起。

春咏

春从何处来？拂水复惊梅。
云障青锁闼，风吹承露台。
美人隔千里，罗帏闭不开。
无由得共语，空对相思杯。

王籍

入若耶溪

舸艎何泛泛，空水共悠悠。
阴霞生远岫，阳景逐回流。
蝉噪林逾静，鸟鸣山更幽。
此地动归念，长年悲倦游。

阴铿

渡青草湖

洞庭春溜满，平湖锦帆张。
沅水桃花色，湘流杜若香。
穴去茅山近，江连巫峡长。
带天澄迥碧，映日动浮光。
行舟逗远树，度鸟息危樯。
滔滔不可测，一苇讵能航？

晚出新亭

大江一浩荡，离悲足几重？
潮落犹如盖，云昏不作峰。
远戍唯闻鼓，寒山但见松。
九十方称半，归途讵有踪？

陈叔宝

玉树后庭花

丽宇芳林对高阁，新妆艳质本倾城。
映户凝娇乍不进，出帷含态笑相迎。
妖姬脸似花含露，玉树流光照后庭。

徐陵

关山月

关山三五月，客子忆秦川。
思妇高楼上，当窗应未眠。
星旗映疏勒，云阵上祁连。
战气今如此，从军复几年？

韦鼎

长安听百舌

万里风烟异，一鸟忽相惊。
那能对远客，还作故乡声。

王褒

渡河北

秋风吹木叶，还似洞庭波。
常山临代郡，亭障绕黄河。
心悲异方乐，肠断陇头歌。
薄暮临征马，失道北山阿。

入关故人别

百年余古树，千里暗黄尘。
关山行就近，相看成远人。

庾信

拟咏怀诗

其二十六

萧条亭障远，凄惨风尘多。
关门临白狄，城影入黄河。
秋风别苏武，寒水送荆轲。
谁言气盖世，晨起帐中歌。

舟中望月

舟子夜离家，开舲望月华。
山明疑有雪，岸白不关沙。
天汉看珠蚌，星桥视桂花。
灰飞重晕阙，蓂落独轮斜。

重别周尚书

阳关万里道，不见一人归。
唯有河边雁，秋来南向飞。

杨广

春江花月夜

暮江平不动，春花满正开。
流波将月去，潮水带星来。

野望

寒鸦飞数点，流水绕孤村。
斜阳欲落处，一望黯销魂。

南北朝民歌

子夜歌

夜长不得眠，明月何灼灼。
想闻散唤声，虚应空中诺。

子夜四时歌 春歌

春林花多媚，春鸟意多哀。
春风复多情，吹我罗裳开。

子夜四时歌 夏歌

青荷盖渌水，芙蓉葩红鲜。
郎见欲采我，我心欲怀莲。

子夜四时歌 秋歌

凉秋开窗寝，斜月垂光照。
中宵无人语，罗幌有双笑。

子夜四时歌 冬歌

渊冰厚三尺，素雪覆千里。
我心如松柏，君情复何似？

西洲曲

忆梅下西洲，折梅寄江北。
单衫杏子红，双鬓鸦雏色。
西洲在何处？两桨桥头渡。
日暮伯劳飞，风吹乌臼树。
树下即门前，门中露翠钿。
开门郎不至，出门采红莲。
采莲南塘秋，莲花过人头。
低头弄莲子，莲子清如水。
置莲怀袖中，莲心彻底红。
忆郎郎不至，仰首望飞鸿。
鸿飞满西洲，望郎上青楼。
楼高望不见，尽日栏杆头。
栏杆十二曲，垂手明如玉。
卷帘天自高，海水摇空绿。
海水梦悠悠，君愁我亦愁。
南风知我意，吹梦到西洲。

木兰诗

唧唧复唧唧，木兰当户织。
不闻机杼声，唯闻女叹息。
问女何所思，问女何所忆。
女亦无所思，女亦无所忆。
昨夜见军帖，可汗大点兵，
军书十二卷，卷卷有爷名。
阿爷无大儿，木兰无长兄，
愿为市鞍马，从此替爷征。

东市买骏马，西市买鞍鞯，
南市买辔头，北市买长鞭。
旦辞爷娘去，暮宿黄河边。
不闻爷娘唤女声，但闻黄河流水鸣溅溅。
旦辞黄河去，暮至黑山头。
不闻爷娘唤女声，但闻燕山胡骑鸣啾啾。

万里赴戎机，关山度若飞。
朔气传金柝，寒光照铁衣。
将军百战死，壮士十年归。

归来见天子，天子坐明堂。
策勋十二转，赏赐百千强。
可汗问所欲，"木兰不用尚书郎，
愿驰千里足，送儿还故乡。"

爷娘闻女来，出郭相扶将。
阿姊闻妹来，当户理红妆。
小弟闻姊来，磨刀霍霍向猪羊。
开我东阁门，坐我西阁床。
脱我战时袍，着我旧时裳。
当窗理云鬓，对镜帖花黄。
出门看火伴，火伴皆惊忙。
同行十二年，不知木兰是女郎。

雄兔脚扑朔，雌兔眼迷离。
两兔傍地走，安能辨我是雄雌。

敕勒歌

敕勒川，阴山下。
天似穹庐，笼盖四野。
天苍苍，野茫茫。
风吹草低见牛羊。

THEORY ON LITERARY TRANSLATION OF THE CHINESE SCHOOL

The theory on literary translation of the Chinese school owes its origin to traditional Chinese culture, including the Confucian and the Taoist school of thought respectively represented by *Thus Spoke the Master* and *Laws Divine and Human*.

It is said in the first chapter of *Laws Divine and Human* that truth can be known, but it may not be the truth you know, and that things may be named, but names are not the things. When applied to literary translation, this may mean that the theory on literary translation can be known, but it may not the unproven theory on the one hand, nor the scientific theory on the other, for neither literary translation nor its theory is science. As the names are not equal to the things, the translation cannot be equal to the original. As there is more difference than equivalence between the Chinese and the English language, the principle of equivalence can not be applied to the translation between them as between two occidental languages.

It is said in the last chapter of *Laws Divine and Human* that truthful words may not be beautiful and beautiful words may not be truthful. That is to say, there is contradiction between truth and beauty or between equivalence and excellence. A translation where equivalents are used may be called a faithful or truthful translation. When no equivalent can be found between two languages, the translator should make use of the best expressions or excellent expressions of the target language. That may be called theory of excellence.

In *Thus Spoke the Master*, Confucius said, "At seventy, I can do what I will without going beyond what is right." Professor Zhu Guangqian said that this has shown the mature state of an artist. I think it may also show the mature state of a literary translator. The literal translator has used the equivalents without going beyond the original in sound; the liberal translator has described the image without going beyond the original in sense; the literary translator has described the scene without going beyond reality. Not to go beyond the original is to be truthful or faithful, and the translator has reached the ordinary level of translation. To do what one will without going beyond the original is not only to be faithful but also to make his translation beautiful, in that case the translator has attained a higher level. To excel the original without going beyond the reality it describes is to attain the highest level.

What is literary translation? It is an art of solving the contradiction between faithfulness (or truth) and beauty. How to solve it? There are three methods, namely, equalization, generalization and particularization. When there is little or no contradition between truth and beauty, equalization or equivalents may be used. When there is contradction between them, generalization may be used to make the meaning clear, and particularization to make a deeper impression.

Confucius said in *Thus Spoke the Master* that it would be good to be understandable, better to be enjoyable and best to be delectable or delightful. When applied to literary translation, this principle means that an understandable translation is good, an enjoyable one is better and a delightful one is best. The ontology or theory of contradition between truth and beauty, the methodology or theory of equalization, generalization and particularization, and the teleology or theory of the understandable, the enjoyable and the delectable, all owe their origin to the Confucian and Taoist schools of thoughts.

But Confucius said less about what delight is and more about how to be delightful. In the beginning of *Thus Spoke the Master* he said it is delightful to acquire knowledge and put it into practice; In Chapter Six he told us how Yan Hui could find delight in reading though living in a humble lane with only a handful of rice to eat and a gourdful of water to drink; In Chapter Eleven, Zeng Xi told us his delight in an spring excursion. From these examples we can see Confucius' theory on delight or teleology, and his theory on practice or methodology. His theory is not scientific but artistic. Since literary translation is an art but not a branch of science, his theory can not only be applied to the practice but also to the theory of literary translation. As his theory has stood the test of time, it is as durable as scientific theories. A theorist on science who studies truth and the truthful should not go beyond what is truthful. A theorist on art or an artist who studies beauty and the beautiful may go beyond what is truthful and faithful.

The contradiction between truth and beauty in Chinese theory on literary translation has developed into a contradiction between equivalence and excellence. As Keats said, "Beauty is truth, truth beauty," we may even say beauty is a virtue, a kind of excellence. When we cannot find the equivalent, we may resort to generalization or particularization.

In short, literary translation is an art to create the beautiful. This is the epistemology of the Chinese school. The contradition between truth and beauty or between equivalence and excellence is its ontology; the theory on equalization, generalization and particularization is its triple methodology; and the theory of the understandable, the enjoyable and the delectable or delightful is its triple teleology.

Xu Yuanchong
Oct. 2011

代后记：中国学派的文学翻译理论

中国学派的文学翻译理论源自中国的传统文化，主要包括儒家思想和道家思想，儒家思想的代表著作是《论语》，道家思想的代表著作是《老子道德经》。

《老子道德经》第一章开始就说："道可道，非常道；名可名，非常名。"联系到翻译理论上来，就是说：翻译理论是可以知道的，是可以说得出来的，但不是只说得出来而经不起实践检验的空头理论，这就是中国学派翻译理论中的实践论。其次，文学翻译理论不能算科学理论（自然科学），与其说是社会科学理论，不如说是人文学科或艺术理论，这就是文学翻译的艺术论，也可以说是相对论。后六个字"名可名，非常名"应用到文学翻译理论上来，可以有两层意思：第一层是原文的文字是描写现实的，但并不等于现实，文字和现实之间还有距离，还有矛盾；第二层意思是译文和原文之间也有距离，也有矛盾，译文和原文所描写的现实之间，自然还有距离，还有矛盾。译文应该发挥译语优势，运用最好的译语表达方式，来和原文展开竞赛，使译文和现实的距离或矛盾小于原文和现实之间的矛盾，那就是超越原文了。这就是文学翻译理论中的优势论或优化论，超越论或竞赛论。文学翻译理论应该解决的不只是译文和原文在文字方面的矛盾，还要解决译文和原文所反映的现实之间的矛盾，这是文学翻译的本体论。

一般翻译只要解决"真"或"信"或"似"的问题，文学翻译却要解决"真"或"信"和"美"之间的矛盾。原文反映的现实不只是言内之意，还有言外之意。中国的文学语言往往有言外之意，甚至还有言外之情。文学翻译理论也要解决译文和原文的言外之意、言外之情的矛盾。

《论语》说："知之者不如好之者，好之者不如乐之者。"知之，好之，乐之，这"三之论"是对艺术论的进一步说明。艺术论第一条原则要求译文忠实于原文所反映的现实，求的是真，可以使人知之；第二条原则要求用"三化"法来优化译文，求的是美，可以使人好之；第三条原则要求用"三美"来优化译文，尤其是译诗词，求的是意美、音美和形美，可以使人乐之。如果"不逾矩"的等化译文能使人知之（理解），那就达到了文学翻译的低标准，如从心所欲而不逾矩的浅化或深化的译文既能使人知之，又能使人好之（喜欢），那就达到了中标准；如果从心所欲的译文不但能使人知之，好之，还能使人乐之（愉快），那才达到了文学翻译的高标准。这也是中国译者对世界译论作出的贡献。

翻译艺术的规律是从心所欲而不逾矩。"矩"就是规矩，规律。但艺术规律却可以依人的主观意志而转移，是因为得到承认才算正确的。所以贝多芬说：为了更美，没有什么清规戒律不可打破。他所说的戒律不是科学规律，而是艺术规律。不能用科学规律来评论文学翻译。

孔子不大谈"什么是"（What?）而多谈"怎么做"（How?）。这是中国传统的方法论，比西方流传更久，影响更广，作用更大，并且经过了两三千年实践的考验。《论语》第一章中说："学而时习之，不亦说（悦，乐）乎！""学"是取得知识，"习"是实践。孔子只说学习实践可以得到乐趣，却不说什么是"乐"。这就是孔子的方法论，是中国文学翻译理论的依据。

总而言之，中国学派的文学翻译理论是研究老子提出的

"信"（似）"美"（优）矛盾的艺术（本体论），但"信"不限原文，还指原文所反映的现实，这是认识论，"信"由严复提出的"信达雅"发展到鲁迅提出"信顺"的直译，再发展到陈源的"三似"（形似，意似，神似），直到傅雷的"重神似不重形似"，这已经接近"美"了。"美"发展到鲁迅的"三美"（意美，音美，形美），再发展到林语堂提出的"忠实，通顺，美"，转化为朱生豪"传达原作意趣"的意译，直到茅盾提出的"美的享受"。孔子提出的"从心所欲"发展到郭沫若提出的创译论（好的翻译等于创作），以及钱钟书说的译文可以胜过原作的"化境"说，再发展到优化论，超越论，"三化"（等化，浅化，深化）方法论。孔子提出的"不逾矩"和老子说的"信言不美，美言不信"有同有异。老子"信美"并重，孔子"从心所欲"重于"不逾矩"，发展为朱光潜的"艺术论"，包括郭沫若说的"在信达之外，愈雅愈好。所谓'雅'不是高深或讲修饰，而是文学价值或艺术价值比较高。"直到茅盾说的："必须把文学翻译工作提高到艺术创造的水平。"孔子的"乐之"发展为胡适之的"愉快"说（翻译要使读者读得愉快），再发展到"三之"（知之，好之，乐之）目的论。这就是中国学派的文学翻译理论发展为"美化之艺术"（"三美"，"三化"，"三之"的艺术）的概况。

许渊冲

2011年10月

图书在版编目（CIP）数据

汉魏六朝诗选：汉英对照 / 许渊冲译. — 北京: 五洲传播出版社,
2018.1（2021.8重印）
（许译中国经典诗文集）
ISBN 978-7-5085-3895-2

Ⅰ.①汉… Ⅱ.①许… Ⅲ.①古典诗歌－诗集－中国－汉代－汉、英
②古典诗歌－诗集－中国－魏晋南北朝时代－汉、英
Ⅳ.①H319.4: I

中国版本图书馆CIP数据核字(2017)第323667号

汉魏六朝诗选

译　　者：许渊冲
策划编辑：荆孝敏　郑　磊
责任编辑：王　峰
中文编辑：赵文平
英文编辑：马培武 程　阳
装帧设计：北京正视文化艺术有限责任公司
出版发行：五洲传播出版社
地　　址：北京市海淀区北三环中路31号生产力大楼B座6层
邮　　编：100088
电　　话：010-82005927，010-82007837
网　　址：http://www.cicc.org.cn http://www.thatsbooks.com
印　　刷：北京市房山腾龙印刷厂
版　　次：2012年1月第1版　2021年8月第2版第3次印刷
开　　本：140mm×210mm 1/32
印　　张：11.25
字　　数：290千字
书　　号：ISBN 978-7-5085-3895-2
定　　价：89.00元